Praise for
The Gospel for Investigators

"Tyler Zach reveals the good news about Enneagram Fives—their unique gifts and contributions to the community—while also addressing the challenges they face and the traps they can fall into. He thoughtfully includes Scripture passages and meditations that affirm and encourage their strengths, along with practical suggestions and spiritual guidance to help Fives climb out of the holes and caves they may have dug for themselves. This book is a valuable resource for understanding the Five within yourself and for loving and supporting the Fives in your life."

— Jerome Wagner, PhD, MDiv, honorary founder of the International Enneagram Association (IEA)

"Jeff and I are thankful the Lord has provided more gospel-centered Enneagram teachers like Tyler Zach. Whether you are new to the Enneagram or have studied it for years, we know that you'll find lasting value in this book. On these pages, Tyler's creative wisdom shines, and his focus always remains on Jesus."

— Beth & Jeff McCord, co-founders of Your Enneagram Coach, best-selling authors of *Becoming Us: Using the Enneagram to Create a Thriving Gospel-Centered Marriage* and *More Than Your Number: A Christ-Centered Enneagram Approach to Becoming AWARE of Your Internal World*

"With a brilliant blend of Scripture, wit, literature, podcast conversations, and insights from competent Enneagram authors, Tyler Zach has crafted a master-level guide for Fives seeking to explore and investigate their inner world. This 40-day journal empowers Fives—and those who love them—to dig deep, reflect, feel, and embrace new ways of thinking, feeling, and engaging with their instincts. I'm confident that my Five students and clients will greatly benefit from this excellent work."

— **Rev. Clare Loughrige, co-author of *Spiritual Rhythms for the Enneagram: A Handbook for Harmony and Transformation,* co-lead pastor of Crossroads Church and Ministries**

" ... A personalized devotional for your personality type. I love it! ... "

— **Les Parrott, PhD, #1 *New York Times* bestselling author of *Saving Your Marriage Before It Starts***

" ... an extraordinary gift to all Enneagram enthusiasts ... "

— **Marilyn Vancil, author of *Self to Lose, Self to Find: Using the Enneagram to Uncover Your True, God-Gifted Self***

" ... Journey through these pages to remember who you are and how to bring your best self to a world in need. ... "

— **Drew Moser, PhD, author of *The Enneagram of Discernment: The Way of Vocation, Wisdom, and Practice***

" ... clear, compelling, and beyond profound."

— **John Fooshee, president of People Launching and Gospel Enneagram**

The Gospel for Investigators

A 40-Day Devotional for Curious, Competent Observers

BY TYLER ZACH

To Kim, my mother and former junior high English teacher, who instilled in me a love for reading and writing, remains my biggest supporter in life, and is the most engaged and generous Five I know.

Table of Contents

When Jeff and I first discovered the Enneagram, it wasn't easy finding books written from a Christian worldview. We understood how important gospel-centered Enneagram resources could be, and that inspired us to start our business, Your Enneagram Coach. Since then, we've helped over one million people find their Type through our free assessment and grow through our online classes, coaching certifications, books, and podcast.

Type Fives are perceptive, innovative, and curious. They engage with the world through observation and analysis, constantly seeking to understand and make sense of everything around them. Their intellectual strength and depth of knowledge are invaluable resources for new ideas and problem-solving. Their emotional stability and ability to remain calm under pressure make them reliable and trusted advisors.

The Enneagram is a tool that clarifies our fallen nature while also reminding us we are created in the *imago Dei* ("image of God"). When Jeff and I understood the why behind our thoughts and actions, it transformed how we looked at ourselves, our relationship with God, our marriage, our parenting, and (obviously) our careers. Taking a risk by starting a business was both exciting and terrifying. We could have easily spun out of control or run out of gas (at times, we did!), but knowing the Enneagram, as seen through the lens of the gospel, kept us grounded and on track.

The world needs Type Fives because your insightful minds and innovative ideas reveal possibilities that others might miss. You bring clarity and understanding to complex issues, helping others navigate uncertainty. Like Christ, you seek truth and offer wisdom to those around you.

Like all numbers, Type Fives have seasons of struggle. Beneath your intellectual strength is a fear of being overwhelmed and depleted. You may withdraw to protect your resources, but this isolation can lead to loneliness and disconnection. A gospel-centered Enneagram can help you see that God enjoys meeting your needs when your energy is low, and sharing your insights with others can enrich your life and the lives of those around you. Type Fives, this 40-day devotional will guide you to the true freedom you desire so you can feel comfortable in the world and find connection and support.

Jeff and I are thankful the Lord has provided more gospel-centered Enneagram teachers like Tyler Zach. Whether you are new to the Enneagram or have studied it for years, we know that you'll find lasting value in this book. On these pages, Tyler's creative wisdom shines, and his focus always remains on Jesus. We're praying that God will meet you on these pages and that you will recognize your inherent value as His beloved child.

Jesus is the author and perfecter of our faith (Hebrews 12:2). He finished the great task He set out to do (John 19:30). A vital part of His ministry was to stay in alignment with His Father, and He did this by setting aside time for rest and reflection. He invites you to do the same, to come away, to separate from the crowds, and be with Him. Remember, you are loved and valued for simply being you. You do not have to gain Christ's approval. You are accepted right now as you are.

—Beth and Jeff McCord
co-founders of Your Enneagram Coach
best-selling authors of *Becoming Us: Using the Enneagram to Create a Thriving Gospel-Centered Marriage* and *More Than Your Number: A Christ-Centered Enneagram Approach to Becoming AWARE of Your Internal World*

The Gospel for Investigators

ARE YOU READY FOR A SELF-DISCOVERY JOURNEY with a labyrinth of endless insights?

Welcome to *The Gospel for Investigators*: an in-depth exploration of your personality type. I promise you that this book is not one of those devotionals filled with inspiring fluff that will make you roll your eyes. Instead, it's a collection of profound insights from dozens of authors and teachers, all filtered through a Christian perspective. Think of this book as a puzzle, providing daily pieces of self-knowledge to help you better understand the complexity of your life and relationships. Often these insights will be so intuitively accurate that it may feel like I'm reading your mail, which can be particularly uncomfortable for Fives, but the good news is you get to reflect on these insights in a safe space before deciding which aha moments to share with others.

Some Fives think that because they don't feel the need to be around other people as much, something must be wrong with them. I'm here to deny this misconception and remind you that you are exactly who God created you to be. At the same time, this book will help you uncover the sources of unhealth in your life: fear and anxiety that come from navigating relationships with loved ones and coworkers who may not understand you. As you walk through each of the forty days, I hope the stress will begin to melt away, allowing you to feel fully seen and appreciated—perhaps for the very first time.

Some people have described Fives as clams: difficult to open but hiding a pearl inside. This book will help you open up more, allowing others to behold your genuine heart and valuable knowledge. We'll also talk about why emotions are so important for improving relationships and decision-making. It's been humorously said that the symbolic plant of a Five is green lettuce because it's "the plant that has its heart in its head."[1] Together, we'll work on bridging the gap between your head and heart!

I had the privilege of being raised by a mother who is a Five. Growing up, I watched her read her Bible in the morning and "win" at Jeopardy every evening! She made sure I was well-prepared for school activities and guided me through college and scholarship applications. As a Nebraska state teacher-of-the-year, she encouraged me to read countless books and helped me excel in state speech meets during high school. She still faithfully attends church every Sunday and exercises supernatural patience as she waits for my Type Two father to finish socializing. Although she has some social anxiety and prefers staying close to home, she remains extremely loyal and generous to her family and close friends. You'll be pleased to know she has already vetted this book, assuring it's worth your time!

What Makes This Book Different?

While other books *explain* the Enneagram, this book's primary aim is to go deeper by applying the truth of God's Word specifically to your type over the next forty days. If you are suspicious of the Enneagram (many Fives are!) or know someone who is, download my free resource called *Should Christians Use the Enneagram?* at gospelforenneagram.com. I pray it will help you engage with this system as a Christian and then talk about it with others.

Before we get to the daily devotions, let's look at how the gospel both affirms and challenges the unique characteristics of your type.

The Gospel Affirms Investigators

God sympathizes with the worldview of an Investigator. In this ignorant and intrusive world, sound wisdom is scarce, overrun by irrational, needy, and demanding people. What we truly need are patient, objective thinkers who can guide us in staying curious, *responding* rather than reacting to life's challenges, processing feelings without getting stuck in them, and innovating future solutions without repeating past mistakes. Your life serves as an example of

---

1   Richard Rohr and Andreas Ebert, *The Enneagram: A Christian Perspective* (New York, NY: The Crossroad Publishing Company, 2001), 116.

someone who illuminates the world with understanding, all while demonstrating great modesty and respect for others. All Investigators will be happy to know the Bible affirms the following beliefs:

- **God created us to be wise and understanding.** "If any of you lacks wisdom, let him ask God, who gives generously to all without reproach, and it will be given him."[2]

- **God created us to think critically and question everything.** "But test everything; hold fast what is good."[3]

- **God created us to cherish moments of solitude.** "And after he had dismissed the crowds, he went up on the mountain by himself to pray. When evening came, he was there alone."[4]

- **God created us to be objective and emotionally stable.** "A hot-tempered man stirs up strife, but he who is slow to anger quiets contention."[5]

- **God created us to explore and study the world.** "But ask the beasts, and they will teach you; the birds of the heavens, and they will tell you; or the bushes of the earth, and they will teach you and the fish of the sea will declare to you."[6]

- **God created us to be thoughtful and discerning.** "The simple believes everything, but the prudent gives thought to his steps."[7]

- **God created us to be prepared and well-reasoned.** "… always being prepared to make a defense to anyone who asks you for a reason for the hope that is in you; yet do it with gentleness and respect."[8]

---

2 James 1:5

3 1 Thessalonians 5:21

4 Matthew 14:23

5 Proverbs 15:18

6 Job 12:7-8

7 Proverbs 14:15

8 1 Peter 3:15

- **God created us to live quietly and mind our own affairs.** "Aspire to live quietly, and to mind your own affairs, and to work with your hands, as we instructed you."[9]

The Gospel Challenges Investigators

The gospel also provides specific challenges to Investigators. We'll explore the most common lies Fives believe and see how the Bible provides much better promises and blessings. We will move deeper into each of these throughout the next forty days.

- **Lie #1: I am loved for being wise and perceptive.** Fives are a gift to the world, reflecting God's *wisdom and truth*. One of their core desires is to be *competent* or "in the know," which is why Fives, like Adam and Eve in the garden, are intrigued by the serpent's alluring offer of intellectual enlightenment.[10] After eating from the Tree of Knowledge of Good and Evil, Fives were separated from God and lost their sense of security in the world, sewing fig leaves to cover up the humiliation of appearing *incompetent*. But the good news is that Jesus died on the cross for your true self, not for the intelligent, well-informed persona you craft. You are not loved for *what* you know but for *who* you know. Because of this, you never have to fear looking foolish in His eyes.

- **Lie #2: Knowledge will make me safe.** Fives often believe their mind is a reliable refuge from the vulnerabilities of the world, leading them to over-pursue knowledge as a path to security. This can foster pride or arrogance, as the apostle Paul warned, "Knowledge puffs up, but love builds up."[11] This relentless quest for knowledge can also cause "monkey mind," a state of restlessness and insomnia. Thus, what Fives perceive as a safe sanctuary can become a mind trap. However, when a Five humbly acknowledges the gaps in their understanding and accepts Christ, they receive the "wisdom of God"[12]—the source of true knowledge and salvation. This liberates them from a state of ignorance and darkened

---

9   1 Thessalonians 4:11

10   Genesis 3:3-5

11   1 Corinthians 8:1

12   1 Corinthians 1:24

understanding. Fives must always remember that productive thinking doesn't originate from the human mind, but rather "the mind of Christ."[13]

- **Lie #3: I can't act unless I know everything.** When Fives lean solely on their own understanding, they block themselves from receiving God's wisdom and guidance.[14] This leads to a false belief that they must fully grasp or master something before taking action, often leaving them trapped in perpetual preparation, telling themselves or others, "I just need to do a little more research." Consequently, they may fall into procrastination rather than moving forward. To overcome this, Fives need to let God redefine their idea of competence from *knowing it all* to *wisdom in action.* Instead of building their foundation solely on their own competence, which is temporary, they should build it on the solid rock of God's wisdom. This means trusting the Holy Spirit's guidance and taking faith-filled risks, even when you don't have everything figured out.

- **Lie #4: Life is better alone.** Fives fear *depletion* of energy and life itself if they remain connected to others, so they raise a drawbridge to avoid feeling overwhelmed by life's demands, seeking refuge in their "mind castle" (or sometimes their literal castle). *Isolation* becomes their defense mechanism for survival, and they may use knowledge as a substitute for the comfort and support found in relationships. While Jesus enjoyed being alone, He wasn't a loner and challenges Fives to *engage* rather than merely observe life from a safe distance. Fives must cultivate the virtue of *non-attachment*, removing unnecessary barriers to freely give and receive in healthy, two-way relationships. When Fives realize God is a more reliable refuge from the challenges of relationships, and that we can draw upon renewed energy each day by abiding in Him, the world won't seem as overwhelming.

- **Lie #5: If I give, I won't get it back.** Fives are often natural minimalists, tending to live below their means and save more than they spend. However, their fear of depletion often leads them to adopt a scarcity mindset, coming to view life as a limited pie and fearing that if someone else takes a piece, there will be less for them. Consequently, unhealthy Fives tend to minimize their own needs and don't afford themselves (or loved ones) many luxuries in life. Their vice, or deadly

---

13   1 Corinthians 2:16

14   Proverbs 3:5-6

sin, is *avarice*, which manifests as hoarding time, energy, affection, or knowledge. While scarcity may lead Fives to believe in a limited pie, the truth is that God can make it bigger. He is not a God of scarcity, providing only a small amount of manna each day, but a God of abundance who delights in giving good gifts to His children.[15] Your needs are never a problem for Him. Living with an abundance mindset demonstrates to others that financial security is not God's highest value; rather, it is generosity.

- **Lie #6: I don't need to depend on anyone.** Another common fear experienced by Fives is the anxiety of feeling *incapable* and *unprepared* to face life's challenges. Instead of relying on others, Fives find it safer and more practical to cultivate independence and self-reliance. However, this strong sense of self-sufficiency can lead to a belief that they don't need much help or the comfort of others. The truth, however, is that no one can do everything alone or provide themselves with every form of comfort they might need. Fives must recognize the strength found within the body of Christ and wholeheartedly embrace the support and vitality of others. Seeking help from others does not indicate weakness; rather, it reflects a healthy trust in God's sufficiency. By embracing *interdependence*, Fives can experience the fullness of life that comes from community and mutual support.

- **Lie #7: Emotions are unpredictable and unreliable.** For Fives, emotions often seem like strangers who show up unexpectedly rather than trusted friends. They struggle to trust feelings because they aren't "facts," and as a result, Fives tend to *compartmentalize*, separating feelings from facts and conveniently storing them away. This is why Fives are often the least emotionally expressive type on the Enneagram. However, cultivating their emotional life will help them become less of a "thinking head on a stick" and more fully human, like Jesus, who embodied the full spectrum of emotions—expressing warmth and love, anger and frustration, grief and loss. When Fives stop "thinking their feelings" and allow emotions to surface, even when they don't make rational sense, they can experience profound transformation in their relationships with the Lord and others.

---

15   Matthew 7:11

As you can see, the gospel will challenge your perception of the protagonists and antagonists in your life. In the Investigator's kingdom, the world is divided into the "competent" and "incompetent": your heroes are those who are intellectually stimulating, predictable, undramatic, and undemanding. They also don't require too much of your time or pressure you to socialize but give you all the autonomy and independence you want. Conversely, your villains are those who stifle your curiosity, invade your privacy, disregard time constraints, make last-minute requests, have excessive emotional needs, or disrupt your alone time.

However, God's kingdom will not be filled with the smart and savvy but by men and women who learned that "the fear of the LORD is the beginning of knowledge."[16] Nicodemus, a prominent Jewish leader in the first century, realized in his late-night conversation with Jesus that entry into this kingdom does not come through intellectual comprehension or right doctrine but through spiritual rebirth. Here, we're invited to encounter God experientially with our hearts, not just our heads. It's a realm where generosity replaces greed, action follows contemplation, theory transitions to practical service, and orthodoxy is surpassed by orthopraxy. In this place, we let go of our need for absolute certainty to embrace the wonder and mystery of God. Skepticism gives way to trust, and passive observers become active participants in God's unfolding plan of redemption.

The Invitation

When Jesus Christ, the divine all in all, entered into flawed and limited human history, He started His mission with an invitation: "The time is fulfilled, and the kingdom of God is at hand; repent and believe in the gospel."[17] He explained that to enter the good, eternally renewing life that begins well before the grave, you must do two things: believe the truth and turn from sin. Believing includes acknowledging who God is, who He says we are, and what He has done for us. More than that, to truly believe in a Christlike way is to *actively live into* those acknowledgments. Turning includes shedding our false worldview, misplaced desires, strong defenses, hide-and-seek strategies, and self-salvation efforts.

---

16   Proverbs 1:7

17   Mark 1:15

If you are ready to begin this incredible forty-day journey and accept God's invitation, then let's get started! It will be an enlightening ride of rapid growth as you become more self-aware and experience newfound freedom. You will encounter many light-bulb moments as you read profound truths for your type—and maybe even learn something about the people around you. The things you learn about yourself in this book will stick with you for the rest of your life.

Three Types of Investigators

To further explore how Fives can look very different from one another, please check out the "Three Types of Investigators" in the back of this book. These "subtypes" are helpful in understanding the nuances of the Investigator and will explain why some truths in this devotional will hit home more than others. If you are a One-to-One Five for example, you will express your emotions more like a Four. Unlike the other Fives who typically tend to me more distant or aloof, the One-to-One Five will be more engaged with loved ones. Therefore, I highly recommend reviewing these brief subtype descriptions first to better understand the unconscious motivations driving your behavior and why you might be mistaken for other Enneagram types.

Day 1:

Stay Curious

Thus says the LORD who made the earth, the LORD who formed it to establish it—the LORD is his name: Call to me and I will answer you, and will tell you great and hidden things that you have not known.

—Jeremiah 33:2-3

HAVE YOU EVER BEEN TOLD THAT YOU ask a lot of questions? Enneagram Fives, the Investigators, are naturally passionate, curious, and inquisitive creatures. Never satisfied with simplistic or superficial answers, this type—more than any other—wants to understand how the world works and why things are the way they are. When looking through a Christ-filtered lens, Investigators intuitively understand that the Universe was constructed with wisdom by a Divine Architect, who engineered everything from the deeply paradoxical and complex relationships of subatomic particles to the deeply paradoxical and intricate relationships between humans!

> I have no special talents. I'm only passionately curious.
>
> –Albert Einstein[1]

---

1 Einstein, Albert. "I have no special talents. I am only passionately curious." Quote Catalog. Accessed May 31, 2024. https://quotecatalog.com/quote/albert-einstein-i-have-no-speci-P1oWvq1.

Ever since then, Fives have been questioning, exploring, and cataloging literally everything they can find.

All Fives have an insatiable hunger for knowledge. As one Five said, "A day without learning is like a day without sunshine."[2] Not that all Fives are doctoral scholars, but rather all are perceptive, generally knowledgeable, and share an incurable curiosity. Fives are rarely motivated by extrinsic goals or accolades, preferring to privately pursue learning for learning's sake and mastering whatever interests them. Often repulsed by intellectual fads, they may explore a niche topic or obscure branch of knowledge over weeks or years for the simple reason that it interests them. And because they don't depend on social validation, they have the internal freedom to tinker with previously accepted doctrines or ways of doing things.

Fives become superfans of their preferred book, author, or series. These allow them to momentarily escape the pressures of the real world while still engaging their intellectual capacities. Author Judith Searle observes that Type Five protagonists in movies are intelligent and observant, using their intellect coolly and unemotionally to solve mysteries, scientific problems, or escape danger.[3] Fives say they are drawn to genres such as science fiction, mysteries, historical fiction, documentaries, biographical pictures, indie films, or anything with intelligent humor.

> Your questions are the key to unraveling cosmic mysteries and expanding human consciousness.

When unhealthy Fives lose their childlike curiosity, their knowledge gains a sharp edge, and they become annoying know-it-alls, making others feel ignorant for their own interests or lack of enlightenment. Healthy Fives, however, cultivate a *humble curiosity*. Unafraid to seem ignorant, they are the first to admit gaps in their knowledge rather than pretending to be omniscient. One example is BibleProject cofounder Jon Collins, who says he enjoys "playing dumb" as a

---

2   Don Richard Riso and Russ Hudson, *The Wisdom of the Enneagram: The Complete Guide to Psychological and Spiritual Growth for the Nine Personality Types* (New York: Bantam Books, 1999), 207.

3   Pace Smith, "Enneagram Story Genres, with Judith Searle." Wild Crazy Meaningful Enneagram. https://pacesmith.com/wcme-028/. Podcast audio, accessed June 9, 2024.

narrator on his illustrated videos because he wants to model what it looks like to stay curious.[4]

The crossroads of spiritual conversion is when a Five must make a decision to trust God's wisdom over their own. As the famous Proverb says, "Trust in the LORD with all your heart, and do not lean on your own understanding. In all your ways acknowledge him, and he will make straight your paths."[5]

Forging your own path in life will feel like navigating an endless *maze* with countless dead ends. However, God invites you into His *labyrinth*, filled with many exciting twists and turns that lead to Him at the center. The labyrinth has a long and complex history with roots dating back to ancient Greece and Rome, but in medieval Christian Europe, labyrinths were often incorporated into the design of cathedrals, such as the beautiful floor of Chartres Cathedral in France. These labyrinths were not designed as puzzles to be navigated but were instead walked as a form of pilgrimage or spiritual practice. Pilgrims would follow the single, continuous path, contemplating their faith and praying as they walked toward the center, where they would reach communion with God.[6]

The Good News for Investigators is that God promises to reward the curious pilgrim. In the book of Jeremiah, God says, "Call to me and I will answer you, and will tell you great and hidden things that you have not known."[7] Take God up on that incredible offer today by embracing your beautiful and inquisitive mind. In doing so, you fulfill your purpose of uncovering the profound beauty that God has woven into the fabric of the universe. Make no mistake: your questions are the key to unraveling cosmic mysteries and expanding human consciousness. Don't be swayed by the opinions of those who might not share your insatiable curiosity, but always go "further up, further in."

---

4   Jesse Eubanks and Lindsey Lewis, "#102: Moving Beyond Type 5's Patterns with Jon Collins of The BibleProject." *RelateBetter*. Podcast audio, October 18, 2023. https://relatebetter.com/102-moving-beyond-type-5-patterns-w-jon-collins-bible-project/.

5   Proverbs 3:5-6

6   John W. Rhodes, "Labyrinths Within the Christian Church Today." Ministry Matters, October 17, 2013. https://www.ministrymatters.com/all/entry/4329/labyrinths-within-the-christian-church-today.

7   Jeremiah 33:3

→ **Pray**

Father, thank You for the gift of curiosity. Let me use it as a source of light and inspiration to everyone around me, revealing the wonders of Your creation. Although You've given me a beautiful mind, help me to not lean on my own understanding but acknowledge You with every step I take on this spiritual pilgrimage.

Day 1 Reflections:

Have you ever been described as someone who asks a lot of questions? How have others perceived and responded to your curious and inquisitive nature?

____

____

____

In what ways has your unending thirst for knowledge manifested throughout the different phases of your life?

____

____

____

Can you recall instances when forging your own path in life felt like moving through an endless maze? How does the concept of exploring God's labyrinth offer a different perspective on your spiritual journey?

____

____

____

→ **Respond**

Search for, listen to, and meditate on the song "Five" from Sleeping At Last.[8]

8   "Atlas: Year Two." *Sleeping At Last*. Accessed June 9, 2024. https://www.sleepingatlast.com/atlas.

Day 2:

A Beautiful Mind

And God gave Solomon wisdom and understanding beyond measure, and breadth of mind like the sand on the seashore, so that Solomon's wisdom surpassed the wisdom of all the people of the east and all the wisdom of Egypt.

—1 Kings 4:29-30

ONE OF THE PLACES I REMEMBER MOST vividly from my childhood is the library. Not the modest building in my small town with its few books—no, my mother would drive my sister and me thirty minutes to "the Mecca" of libraries (for rural Northeast Nebraska, anyway). This regular pilgrimage for our family gave me an early appreciation for the importance of knowledge and reading. I still remember how my mother's nightstand held a stack of books with far too many to be consumed within the confines of a single rental period.

> A room without books is like a body without a soul.
>
> —Marcus Tullius Cicero[1]

Fives like my mother are bookish creatures who, like archeologists, dig up and painstakingly brush through questions to uncover mysteries

---

1 "A Quote by Marcus Tullius Cicero." Goodreads. Accessed June 15, 2024. https://www.goodreads.com/quotes/764-a-room-without-books-is-like-a-body-without-a.

and secrets under the surface. As the American astronomer Carl Sagan said, "Understanding is a kind of ecstasy."[2]

There is no limit to the range of subjects a Five will explore. As the famous mathematician and philosopher Blaise Pascal explains, "Since we cannot be universal and know all that is to be known of everything, we ought to know a little about everything."[3] It's fascinating to me that the average Five loathes spending money on their own comfort and clothing but will use much of their modest budget on acquiring more knowledge and skills.[4] Why? Because *knowledge* is a Five's currency.

Knowledge is more valuable than money. When Fives feel intelligent, well-informed, and competent, it makes them feel more confident around others, more in control of their environment, and more comfortable in the world. In other words, being "in the know" makes connecting with others and life in general feel a little less overwhelming. Zooming out, Fives place such value on knowledge because they believe *ideas change the world*. Look no further than the great philosophers Plotinus, Thomas Aquinas, Bonaventure, Descartes, and Spinoza—all of whom changed the way we think about the world and our place in it.

> Acquiring knowledge isn't just for fun but for making an impact on the world around you.

The word *philosophy* comes from the Greek word *philosophos* which literally means "lover of wisdom."[5] The typical Western philosophy textbook will open with ancient Greece in the sixth century BC, but five centuries before lived a man named Solomon, son of the great King David. The Lord appeared to Solomon in a dream one night shortly after his ascension to the throne of Israel, and said, "Ask what I shall give you."[6] Solomon answered by saying his greatest desire, above

---

2   Ian Morgan Cron and Suzanne Stabile, *The Road Back to You: An Enneagram Journey to Self-Discovery* (Downers Grove, IL: InterVarsity Press Books, 2016), 173.

3   Riso and Hudson, *The Wisdom of the Enneagram*, 205.

4   Don Riso and Russ Hudson, *Personality Types: Using the Enneagram for Self-Discovery* (New York, NY: Houghton Mifflin Company Books, 1996), 187-188.

5   Dictionary.com. "Philosophy." Accessed May 31, 2024. https://www.dictionary.com/browse/philosophy.

6   1 Kings 3:5

all jewels or victories in war, was to acquire "a wise and discerning mind."[7] God was pleased with this unique request and made him the wisest person on the earth—and offered the rest as a bonus.[8] People from every nation, including the famous Queen of Sheba, traveled many months to sit under (and be impressed by) Solomon's wisdom. A Five's dream! This impressive wisdom and breadth of knowledge, and high level of influence Solomon was able to exert on the world can be traced back to his core conviction that "wisdom is better than jewels, and all that you may desire cannot compare with her."[9]

The Good News for Investigators is like Solomon, "If any of you lacks wisdom, let him ask God, who gives generously to all without reproach, and it will be given him."[10] For instance, God loved pouring out wisdom on the Bereans, a group of Jewish people living in first century Macedonia. They were critical thinkers and diligent students of the Hebrew Scriptures, and were commended for their daily habit of examining the writings to verify the truth of what the apostle Paul preached during his visits there.[11]

Like the Bereans, God commends you for your positive example of seeking the truth through careful examination. He loves when you don't simply take someone's word but "test everything,"[12] as Paul exhorted us to do. God wants you to use that beautiful mind of yours to push back ignorance, expose falsehoods, innovate, and alter history's course. Never let the incurious cause you to underestimate the power of knowledge: having more of it doesn't make you superior but a useful instrument in God's hands. Remember, acquiring knowledge isn't just for fun but for making an impact on the world around you.

---

7 1 Kings 3:12

8 1 Kings 4:29-31

9 Proverbs 8:11

10 James 1:5

11 Acts 17:10-15

12 1 Thessalonians 5:21

> **→ Pray**
>
> Father, from Your mouth comes knowledge and understanding.[13] Like Solomon, I'm grateful for the wealth of knowledge You've woven into my life. Like the Bereans, I will continue to study and examine Your Word with diligence. Help me remember that knowledge is not just for personal joy but an instrument for positive change in this world.

Day 2 Reflections:

In what ways has acquiring knowledge brought more confidence, control, and comfort to your life and relationships?

When have you been commended or critiqued for being a seeker and examiner of truth? How has this affected your spiritual journey for better or worse?

Which specific insights do you currently hold that you believe have the potential to positively change the lives of those around you?

> **→ Respond**
>
> Share an intriguing fact or insight with someone else today to create a shared moment of discovery and amplify your joy of knowledge.

---

13 Proverbs 2:6

The Castle

Behold, I stand at the door and knock. If anyone hears my voice and opens

the door, I will come in to him and eat with him, and he with me.

—Revelation 3:20

ACCLAIMED CREATOR OF VEGGIETALES, PHIL VISCHER ONCE shared his dream as a young boy, where he would construct his very own fortress on his grandpa's vast land in rural Michigan. In a recent interview, Phil shared the deep-seated desire for the security and self-containment that a castle symbolizes. They offer security against pillaging hoards or, as he mentioned, protection from wandering bears. "Life is full of bears," Phil mused, noting that there are many people who want to consume his time and resources.[2]

> When afraid, Fives tend to pull away from connections with others while trying to work out everything in their heads.
>
> —Suzanne Stabile[1]

---

1   Suzanne Stabile, *The Journey Toward Wholeness: Enneagram Wisdom for Stress, Balance, and Transformation* (Downers Grove, IL: InterVarsity Press, 2021), 73.

2   Jesse Eubanks and Lindsey Lewis, "#91: Your Desire to Be Competent with Phil Vischer (Type 5)." The EnneaCast. Podcast audio, May 16, 2023. https://podcasts.apple.com/us/podcast/91-your-desire-to-be-competent-w-phil-vischer-type-5/id1410031710?i=1000613215985.

The desire to be locked up and safe in their fortress reflects a yearning for Fives, especially the Self-Preservation subtype, to shield themselves from the unpredictable and potentially threatening elements in their lives. While others seem to be annoyingly comfortable living in a world full of surprises, many Fives experience some level of social insecurity.

All Fives fear being *engulfed by the demands of others*, believing that some people are like "black holes," sucking you into their vortex of emotions and needs. It's no wonder this type plays possum when those overly energetic extroverts come around, retreating into their secure tortoise shells, as Ian Cron describes.[3] Enneagram pioneer Claudio Naranjo likened an overwhelmed Five to a cuttlefish that lives in the crevices of rocks alone and ejects ink for camouflage when threatened.[4]

For healthy Fives, the inclination to pull up the drawbridge is not usually about avoiding life's complexities but rather about navigating them from a position of greater power and strength. When conflict arises or hurt occurs, they withdraw to the castle to process from a safe distance.

> Fives fear being engulfed by the demands of others.

Establishing genuine connections might have been challenging for you when growing up. People were either too intrusive or too unavailable, leading to the preference for solitude. You likely concluded that *avoiding* most social interactions requires far less energy than engaging and have made a habit of retreating into your head or home. You seek refuge in your metaphorical or literal castle, a haven with minimal interruptions or social inconveniences, where you could be yourself without feeling inadequate or different.

Yet, as you may have encountered, the inclination to withdraw from the real world can lead to a lapse in recognizing the significance of human connections. It's essential to acknowledge that we were intricately wired by God with a fundamental need for these connections—yearning for emotional support,

---

3   Ian Morgan Cron, *The Story of You: An Enneagram Journey to Becoming Your True Self* (New York, NY: HarperCollins, 2021), 151.

4   Claudio Naranjo, *Character and Neurosis: An Integrative View* (Nevada City, CA: Gateways/IDHHB, 1994), 95.

empathy, compassion, and a sense of belonging. While it may feel safer, retreating to your castle and pulling up the drawbridge is often counterproductive as it not only bars entry to those who might bring harm but also excludes those who want to offer you their genuine support.

The Good News for Investigators is that Jesus stands at the drawbridge, gently knocking, asking to enter and bring His calm, life-giving presence. Just like He did for the church at Laodicea that had grown lukewarm, neither offering the refreshing waters of life nor healing warmth, Jesus extends an invitation to all Fives to turn away from relational and spiritual complacency. He's asking you to lower your drawbridge and allow Him and even the world inside for companionship. But fear not, opening up doesn't automatically unleash the floodgates; you can trust that Jesus will be your protective barrier and stronghold, a shield from the challenges and uncertainties that come with being in relationships. He's got you covered!

→ Pray

Father, help me to balance solitude and connection. When I begin pulling up the drawbridge, reveal my fears and give me the courage to overcome them. Because You are my refuge and shield wherever I go, I will open myself up and receive the sweet gift of fellowship with You and companionship with others who have my best in mind.

Day 3 Reflections:

How does the metaphor of building a castle resonate with your desire for comfort and security? Can you relate to the idea of creating a haven where you feel protected from life's challenges?

Reflect on the challenges mentioned regarding people feeling either too intrusive or too unavailable. How did these experiences shape your inclination to withdraw?

Are there specific situations where you find yourself instinctively pulling up the drawbridge? What lingering fears do you need to overcome in order to lower your drawbridge and open yourself up to greater companionship?

→ Respond

Invite someone into your personal space. Whether by sharing more of your thoughts and feelings or welcoming them into your home, offer a glimpse into your private world.

Day 4:

Beyond Observation

Oh, taste and see that the LORD is good! Blessed

is the man who takes refuge in him!

—Psalm 34:8

INVESTIGATORS ARE THE OWLS OF THE ENNEAGRAM. Throughout history and in various cultures, owls have been symbols of wisdom and knowledge: for instance, the ancient Greeks chose the owl as the symbol for their goddess of wisdom, Athena. Similarly, Fives are master observers, sitting on their perches, taking in their surroundings with extraordinary perception. Nothing escapes their notice; they delight in discovering details and interesting facts that others might miss. They have an insatiable curiosity and can never allow an unanswered question to float away without, well, *investigating.*

> I have always thought the actions of men the best interpreters of their thoughts.
>
> –John Locke[1]

Just as an owl is known for its patience while hunting, Fives are

---

1 L. A. Selby-Bigge, *British Moralists: Samuel Clarke. Balguy. Richard Price. Appendix: Balguy. Brown. John Clarke. Cudworth. John Gay. Hobbes. Kames. Locke. Mandeville. Paley. Wollaston* (United Kingdom: Clarendon Press, 1897), 328.

thoughtful and strategic and deliberately wait for extended periods of time before they act. When they are on the move, they fly silently, minimizing any noise that might give away their presence, remaining composed in stressful situations, and responding rather than reacting.

Fives prefer to *observe* rather than *participate*, which can lead to misconceptions and unfair labels such as "loner" or "antisocial," a notion that is far from accurate. When in the company of those they're comfortable with, or individuals who share their passion for specific interests or hobbies, Fives can actually be very sociable and engaging. Still, their comfort with being alone and penchant for not taking part in common activities sometimes leads to assumptions that they're not enjoying themselves or are mentally checked out. These assumptions are typically incorrect: Fives simply have their own ways of finding fulfillment, which don't necessarily align with more conventional forms of socializing.

> Life cannot be fully grasped through observation alone but requires direct participation to truly understand.

However, an important growth area for this type involves *participating* in life's experiences rather than merely observing from the sidelines. They may overlook the fact that they were created to be players, not just spectators. Fives might feel the need to thoroughly understand the "rules of the game" before they feel ready to step onto the field, often resulting in them observing for longer than necessary. But they should never forget that the point is to *play the game*.[2]

Life cannot be fully grasped through observation alone but requires direct participation to truly understand. This juxtaposition is seen in two of the greatest thinkers in Western history, René Descartes and John Locke. Descartes, the renowned seventeenth-century French philosopher, preferred observation and believed in acquiring knowledge through reasoning alone, epitomized in his maxim, "I think, therefore I am," which on one level indicates that the very presence of rational thought was proof enough of life. Descartes chose to live in

---

2   Jerome Peter Wagner, *Nine Lenses on the World: The Enneagram Perspective* (Evanston, IL: NineLens Press, 2010), 310.

seclusion in Holland, valuing the anonymity it provided and believing it would be better to be unseen and unbothered by others. In contrast, John Locke, a proponent of British empiricism, argued that true knowledge and proof of life stems not solely from the intellect but from experience and sensory engagement with the world.[3] The difference in their viewpoints suggests that, just as Descartes might have benefited from embracing some of Locke's ideas, so too can Fives gain from considering a more experiential approach to life.

The Good News for Investigators is that you are invited to know God experientially, not just intellectually. As the psalmist proclaimed, "Taste and see that the LORD is good."[4] Just as tasting food allows us to experience its flavor directly, "tasting" in a spiritual sense is an invitation to have a direct, sensory experience of God and the abundant life He offers. It suggests having the willingness to open yourself up to new experiences, allowing the goodness of God to fill your senses, much like a delightful dish satiates our palate. This invitation is a reminder that the abundant life is meant to be *lived*, not just *studied*.[5] Take up God's offer to move from passive observation to active participation to enjoy a more deeply satisfying existence. You'll never *know* until you try!

→ Pray

Father, I praise You for blessing me with keen observation and insatiable curiosity, allowing me to appreciate the intricacies of Your creation. Help me to balance this gift with the courage to actively participate in the life You've given me. Thank You for the opportunity to taste and see Your goodness in every moment.

---

3   Peter Markie and M. Folescu. "Rationalism vs. Empiricism." Stanford Encyclopedia of Philosophy, September 2, 2021. https://plato.stanford.edu/ENTRIES/rationalism-empiricism/.

4   Psalm 34:8

5   Riso and Hudson, *The Wisdom of the Enneagram*, 229-230.

Day 4 Reflections:

Can you recall a moment when you transitioned from being an observer to a participant, and it led to a deeper understanding or knowledge?

Reflecting on the contrasting philosophies of Descartes and Locke, where do you find yourself on the spectrum between relying on reason and experience to learning about the world?

Where in your life do you need to engage more actively right now, and what opportunities might you miss if you remain on the sidelines?

➜ Respond

Choose an area or activity where you've been on the sidelines—be it your church, a spiritual practice, or deepening connections with friends or family. Decide when and how you will actively engage in this chosen area this week.

For this reason I remind you to fan into flame the gift of God,

which is in you through the laying on of my hands, for God gave

us a spirit not of fear but of power and love and self-control.

—2 Timothy 1:6-7

ONE OF MY FAVORITE TELEVISION SERIES GROWING up was the brilliant and ever-resourceful *MacGyver.* Known for his ability to evade trouble using unconventional methods, MacGyver captivated me with his ability to defuse a bomb with a paper clip or hot-wire a car with a chocolate bar. He never carried a lethal weapon, but when trouble came knocking, he was always armed with duct tape. I didn't know it at the time, but this ingenious childhood hero of mine was an Investigator. This unique type of hero wasn't a "shoot first, ask questions later" type, but he also didn't sit safely in HQ, keeping his knowledge to himself. His resourcefulness and calm demeanor

> It's not that I'm so smart, it's just that I stay with problems longer.
>
> —Albert Einstein[6]

---

6 Drew Moser, *The Enneagram of Discernment: The Way of Vocation, Wisdom, and Practice* (Beaver Falls, PA: Falls City Press, 2020), 301.

made him exactly the sort of hero you wanted navigating complex missions with lives hanging in the balance.

In his second letter to young Timothy, the apostle Paul challenged his student in the faith not to remain passive with the knowledge he possessed. He exhorted Timothy to "fan into flame" his God-given strengths. He was concerned that his protégé could—as we all do occasionally—become complacent, allowing his presence and contributions to become lethargic or dormant. An attentive reader of the apostle's letter might ask themselves, "What would it look like for me to 'fan into flame the gift of God'?"[7]

At the top of the list of Five's strengths is the ability to stay rational and objective in the middle of a storm. When they are surrounded by hot-headed, irrational fools, they parse out the emotions from ideas, remaining logical, grounded, and able to make clear-headed decisions without getting caught in emotional entanglements. Extremely patient as a rule, Fives count the cost, building from the ground up with integrity and not succumbing to the pressure to take shortcuts. More than any other type, Fives *respond* rather than *react* to life.

> Fives respond rather than react to life.

Thoughtful and careful, they can concentrate on complex issues or problems for long periods of time. They research the situation from every possible angle, then emerge from their cave of solitude with well-reasoned arguments that are hard to argue with or disprove. Their ability to analyze and summarize data helps us make better decisions and gives us useful information to be more practical in our fields. Their high-level comprehension skills also allow them to make correlations where others only see confusion and make predictions long before anyone can validate them. But because healthy Fives are professional and modest, they don't let their own ego or emotions get in the way, which gives them the ability to produce largely unbiased work.

A Five's natural neutrality allows them to consider many viewpoints at once without being attached to any. Desiring knowledge over approval and substance over style, they want to know how the world works more than they want to be

---

7   2 Timothy 1:6

applauded by it. This willingness to work for love of knowledge itself also makes them trustworthy teachers or team leaders.

Fives are innovative and inventive, though they don't always set out to walk on the moon. Mostly, they just want to explore uncharted territories, finding joy in the hunt of new learning. Unsatisfied with the status quo or conventional approaches, they are always seeking novel ways of doing everyday things. When they make discoveries, find inconsistencies, or come across exceptions to the rules, they find joy in sharing these findings with others.[8]

The Good News for Investigators is that Christ's love enflames your capacity to be curious, perceptive, thoughtful, objective, focused, and highly independent. Your natural gifts are part of a grand plan to restore humanity, mirroring Christ's example of setting our minds free to pursue both the logical ends of this endlessly complex universe He created, as well as mysterious, deeper, spiritual truths.[9] The way you pursue Jesus in stillness and solitude, seeking depth of wisdom and clarity in His presence, will help all of us find liberation from ignorance and stimulate spiritual growth.

→ Pray

Father, like Timothy's mother and grandmother, I wouldn't be here without my friends and family. Thank You for giving me faithful people who have strengthened my faith and encouraged me to fan into flame the gifts You've given me. Help me to spread the flames of truth, while remaining wise and calm, putting out fires started by foolish people.

---

8   Riso and Hudson, *The Wisdom of the Enneagram*, 228-229.

9   John 8:31-32

Day 5 Reflections:

Reflecting on the description of the Five's strengths, which ones have been affirmed the most in your life?

What are some examples of how you are presently applying your gifts in various areas of your life?

→ Respond

Choose one gift and determine how you will consistently practice, refine, cultivate and use it in your daily life.

Day 6:
The Tree of Knowledge

But God said, "You shall not eat of the fruit of the tree that is in the midst of the garden, neither shall you touch it, lest you die." But the serpent said to the woman, "You will not surely die. For God knows that when you eat of it your eyes will be opened, and you will be like God, knowing good and evil."

—Genesis 3:3-5

DO YOU REALIZE OTHERS CAN SEE GOD more clearly through your personality? God created all of us as "mirrors" to reflect different aspects of His heart and character to a broken, hurting world. All of us are truly the *imago Dei*, translating the infinite, invisible One for a finite, visible world. When walking in the Spirit, you are curious, insightful, interesting, witty, objective, observant, perceptive, thoughtful, respectful, rational, and knowledgeable.

> Infinite knowledge can never wonder. All wonder is the effect of novelty upon ignorance.
>
> –Dr. Samuel Johnson[1]

Pause for a moment and read that list again. You are a remarkable reflection of God's wisdom and truth. As spiritual director and

---

1 Irving Babbitt, *Rousseau and Romanticism* (Boston, MA: Houghton Mifflin, 1924), 50.

Enneagram author Marilyn Vancil teaches, "Those who identify with Type Five reflect God's wisdom and a deep inner knowing that illuminates the mind and heart. They are keen observers who are able to bring forth simplicity in the midst of life's complexities. When they experience moments of clear understanding, they sense a holy awe at belonging to profound truth. As one who is connected to the wisdom of God, they long to comprehend the deeper realities of life and apply this knowledge for the sake of living well in the world."[2]

But as you know, it's impossible to reflect those characteristics of God at all times. The apostle Paul said the mirror was cracked from top to bottom when we exchanged the glory of God for the glory of man.[3]

> You are a remarkable reflection of God's wisdom and truth.

And it's not even a mistake relegated to people of the past, but like all wrongs perpetrated by humans, it's something we all *still do*. When walking in the flesh, those positive attributes turn sour, and you will find yourself moving away from the list of attributes of walking in the Spirit toward being withdrawn, reclusive, uncommunicative, obsessive, uncaring, cheap, heady, antagonistic, self-reliant, cynical, and avoidant of commitment.

This pattern of exchanging God's glory for our own idea of it can all be traced back to that tragic scene in the garden of Eden. In our innocent home stood the Tree of the Knowledge of Good and Evil, of whose fruit God commanded Adam and Eve to never eat. But a crafty serpent slithered into their minds and sowed doubt, tempting Adam and Eve with the allure of *forbidden knowledge*. Unable to resist, they took a bite, ushering in sin and separation from a benevolent God who promised to meet all their needs.

Even if you don't desire to be *omniscient* like God, all Investigators are still tempted to cover themselves with knowledge's fig leaves to protect themselves from that horrible feeling of *incompetence*. The humiliation due to a lack of knowledge triggers the Type Five's greatest fear: appearing foolish, unprepared,

---

2   Marilyn Vancil, *Self to Lose, Self to Find: Using the Enneagram to Uncover Your True, God-gifted Self* (New York: Convergent, 2020), 98.

3   Romans 1:23

unintelligent, incapable, or inadequate.[4]   That's why you might feel this gravitational pull to keep researching: because you are afraid someone is going to ask you a question you don't have the answer for, just how as a child, you may have felt insecure, stupid, or embarrassed at times when you drew a complete blank or were caught off guard with a question.[5]

When you drift from the gospel promise that you are worthy because of Christ, you will work hard to present a preferred image to the world that says, "I am useful because I am wise and perceptive."[6] When unhealthy, you become a master sculptor, picking up the chisel and carving the perfect well-informed persona that is observant, astute, and reserved rather than unaware, gullible, and stupid. You are tempted to believe the world rewards those who are knowledgeable and self-sufficient, so you keep running on the treadmill of learning long after your legs and lungs are tired.

The Good News for Investigators is Jesus died on the cross for you—for your ignorant self, not your intelligent, studious, crafted self. You are not loved for *what* you know but *who* you belong to. You are, right now without any effort, the *imago Dei*. Remember, *competence does not equal influence*—the blue-collar disciples, Peter and John, astonished others not because they were educated but because "they had been with Jesus."[7] In other words, as the expression goes, "It's not what you know, but who you know" that truly matters. Today, don't rejoice in the fact that you are more informed than others but that your name is written in heaven.[8]

---

4   Cron and Stabile, *The Road Back to You*, 173-174.

5   Vancil, *Self to Lose, Self to Find*, 100.

6   Wagner, *Nine Lenses on the World*, 308.

7   Acts 4:13

8   Luke 10:20

→ Pray

Father, relax my tendency to portray a competent and self-sufficient image. Help me to be more vulnerable with my inadequacies and ineptitudes. Like Adam and Eve, pursue me when I isolate in fear. Open my ears to hear Your voice calling me out of hiding, inviting me to replace my fragile fig leaves with the covering of Your belovedness.

Day 6 Reflections:

Which of these words most reflect the image of God in you: curious, insightful, interesting, witty, objective, observant, perceptive, thoughtful, respectful, rational, and knowledgeable?

When did you start to believe the lie "I'm more useful when I'm wise and perceptive"? What people or life experiences have reinforced that belief?

How do you relate to the fear of incompetency—appearing foolish, unprepared, unintelligent, incapable, or inadequate? How does the gospel offer relief from this fear?

→ Respond

When someone asks you a question, don't unload everything you know in an attempt to appear competent. In humility, share your knowledge in moderation.[9]

---

9   Adele Ahlberg Calhoun, Douglas A. Calhoun, Clare M. Loughrige, and Scott Loughrige, *Spiritual Rhythms For The Enneagram: A Handbook for Harmony and Transformation* (Downers Grove, IL: InterVarsity Press, 2019), 145-146.

The Compassionate Thinker

By this all people will know that you are my disciples,

if you have love for one another.

—John 13:35

AN ANCIENT TWELVE-YEAR-OLD BOY ONCE FOUND HIMSELF in a situation eerily similar to the classic movie *Home Alone*. Imagine the scene as his parents, much like the hurried family in the Christmas comedy, unwittingly left their son behind after an annual cultural celebration. Assuming their boy was with their family's group, they traveled a whole day's journey before realizing their mistake. Frantic and scared, they took the first flight (or donkey) back to rescue their presumably terrified, lonely child.[2]

> I used to think being loved was the greatest thing to think about, but now I know love is never satisfied just thinking about it.
>
> —Bob Goff[1]

It took these anxious parents, Joseph and Mary, three whole days to find

---

1 Bob Goff, *Love Does: Discover a Secretly Incredible Life in an Ordinary World* (Nashville, TN: Thomas Nelson, 2012), 17.

2 Luke 2:41-45

their boy in the bustling metropolis of Jerusalem, but to their great surprise, Jesus, like Kevin McCallister, had enjoyed much of His time alone. They didn't find their child in distress but rather sitting in the temple, engaging scholars with profound questions and offering His own insights. The adults in the room were taken aback by this boy who was wise beyond His years.[3]

Jesus' early intellectual curiosity is just one of many characteristics mirrored by the traits of the Investigator personality type. Jesus was inquisitive from birth and possessed the ability to analyze and synthesize vast amounts of Scripture. Luke's Gospel displays this well, as we see Jesus interpreting the entire arc of the Jewish Scriptures in light of Himself, and then we see His remarkable ability to pick up on unspoken things in conversation: "When Jesus perceived their thoughts, he answered them, 'Why do you question in your hearts?'"[4] As a fun side note, the "orderly accounting" gospel writer Luke is considered by many to be the Five's doppelganger.

> Jesus cared more about hearts than heads.

Jesus was a revered teacher, imparting profound wisdom to crowds. The Sermon on the Mount emerges as a particularly noteworthy illustration of Jesus challenging prevailing Scriptural interpretations of the time and introducing new and groundbreaking insights.[5] Like a Five, Jesus maintained a calm composure when having to deal with the Pharisees, those foolish leaders who drained all His energy, and later, His life. Yet rather than lashing out at these deaf and blind spiritual shepherds, He outwitted them with His intellect.

Jesus probably felt engulfed often by people who just wouldn't leave Him alone—demanding another healing, miraculous sign, sermon, or selfie. But in Five-like fashion, He often distanced Himself from the crowds to get silence and solitude with His Father. Make no mistake: though Jesus enjoyed being alone, He wasn't a loner. His time of solitude was not an end in itself but fuel to prepare Him for loving compassion.[6] While Jesus stands out as the wisest person in history,

---

3   Luke 2:46-52

4   Luke 5:22

5   Jesse Eubanks, *How We Relate: Understanding God, Yourself, and Others Through the Enneagram* (Grand Rapids, MI: Zondervan, 2023), 170.

6   Ibid., 171.

He is predominantly remembered not as an intellectual figure but as a man with compassion.

Do you prioritize the needs of people first? Do you find yourself more captivated by ideas than by the individuals expressing them? Jesus cared more about *hearts* than heads. He didn't allow Himself to get caught up in heady conversations and arguments over minutiae, turning people into issues, but rather observed the real emotional and physical needs of real people first.

The litmus test of being a true disciple is not how much you know, read the Bible, or memorize Scripture but whether you display a heart of compassion. Jesus knew the potential for intellectual pride and arrogance, as well as the accolades pursuing such things could gain for Him, yet He always emphasized the importance of love as the primary ingredient in drawing people to God.

The Good News for Investigators is when you're low on energy and don't feel capable of love, Jesus assures you that He can fill you with compassion. If you prioritize abiding in Him over burying yourself in books, the world will recognize you first and foremost as a lover, not a thinker. Breathe in deeply, then let out a sigh of relief. Love doesn't have to be a tiring external pursuit nor a topic to master—rather, it is simply an internal fruit of the Spirit we can cultivate and tend.[7] A greater capacity to love doesn't stem from your efforts alone, but from being connected to the true source: the Vine.[8]

→ Pray

Father, as the world often demands my attention and leaves me feeling drained, help me value solitude not as an end in itself but as fuel for loving compassion. Give me discernment to prioritize the needs of people over captivating ideas, following Jesus' example of caring more about hearts than heads.

---

7   Galatians 5:22-23

8   John 15:5

Day 7 Reflections:

Consider how Jesus balanced curiosity and compassion. Who have you shown remarkable compassion to by becoming the hands and feet of Jesus?

Assess your priorities: Are you more drawn to ideas or the needs of individuals? How can you balance intellectual pursuits with genuine care for others?

How will you prioritize abiding in Jesus without neglecting your intellectual pursuits? What might that look like for you on a practical level?

> ### → Respond
>
> Identify someone who needs more care than curiosity from you today. Show them tangible love through a meaningful gesture or action.

Express Your Emotions

Jesus wept.

—John 11:35

IMAGINE BEING INVITED TO AN ANCIENT LIBRARY, brimming with rare and precious manuscripts. But when you arrive, you discover the front entrance is sealed. Inquiring about the visiting hours, you learn the library unlocks its doors for just one hour at random times throughout the month. How would that leave you feeling? Fives are that library: full of mysterious knowledge, waiting for someone to arrive who will truly appreciate browsing the shelves (quietly, of course!), patiently hunting through hidden troves of deep thought. Yet all too often, the doors are barred, and the times they might be flung open are as hidden as the treasure held within.

> The emotion that can break your heart is sometimes the very one that heals it.
>
> —Nicholas Sparks[1]

What God intended for Fives to lend to the public, they've put under lock and key in their private vault. Fives' emotional range is as broad as anyone's, but they are typically the

---

1 X.Com." X (formerly Twitter). Accessed June 17, 2024. https://x.com/NicholasSparks/status/1762890127804678382.

least emotionally *expressive* of all the Types (with the exception of the One-to-One Five subtype). You'll rarely see a Five display big emotions in public, except when there is passion around intellectual points of interest.[2]

Why is it so hard for Fives to be more expressive? They prefer to keep feelings private at first, putting them under a microscope for analysis before they are willing to put them on display. Feelings don't often feel like friends but lingering strangers who interrupt in strange and unexpected ways. These intrusions may cause the average Five actual physical discomfort or at least a desire to protect themselves from the unwanted "guests." From the Five's point of view, other Types seem to have a much more natural capacity to express and relate to feelings.

Another challenge of this delayed emotional analysis is that feelings usually aren't allowed to hit them in the present. They may look and feel emotionally steady in the moment, but then get a visit from grief in the middle of

> Jesus was a kaleidoscope of emotions, able to express the entire spectrum of human warmth and love, anger and frustration, grief and loss.

the night a few days later—and the cost of dealing with these delayed emotions can run high. As one Five shared, "Processing comes with a price. I am usually exhausted for several days afterward. It has been a life-long struggle to come out of hiding."[3] Once family members and friends understand this about Fives, we can begin to have more empathy for these alternating seasons of perceived emotional stasis followed by deep exhaustion.

Jim Cofield, director of CrossPoint Ministry, tells his fellow Fives that their *emotional needs are not a problem*. It may seem that you might overwhelm others if they see the deep expanse of emotions under the tip of the iceberg, but more often than not, they won't. Don't try to "figure out" your emotions through sheer analytical force but rather bring them in the present to the Lord and to others you trust. Just like someone has to start babbling when they are learning a new

---

2   Beatrice Chestnut, *The 9 Types of Leadership: Mastering the Art of People in the 21st Century Workplace* (Post Hill Press, 2017), 170.

3   Calhoun and Loughrige, *Spiritual Rhythms*, 133.

language, so too must we learn to express our feelings even before they make any rational sense.[4]

Rather than packing up your feelings for later, channeling them into fantasies, or translating them into binary code to neutralize, practice holding space for them. When your body communicates through fiery sensations, blow on the embers to ignite those emotions, and add even more fuel to the fire. Nurture these feelings and let others join you; they don't need to know the fire's origin—just let them in the circle of its warmth. Sitting with your emotions and sharing them in real time can transform your relationships. When captivated by beauty or sadness, just cry. It's that simple. Don't waste your tears; use them to nourish your soul and relationships.

The Good News for Investigators is that Jesus was a kaleidoscope of emotions, able to express the entire spectrum of human warmth and love, anger and frustration, grief and loss. When we say that Jesus was "fully human," we mean that He experienced it all—only more so. He felt deep compassion toward the sick and infirm, anger toward evil and hypocrisy, grief over death and loneliness, and distress over humanity's waywardness. Jesus' message to you today is that *love transcends mere understanding*; it's a profound experience, a force to be deeply felt and lived out.

→ Pray

Father, help me to express my emotions as freely as Jesus did, from joy and compassion to sorrow and frustration. Help me unlock my heart, sharing its depths not as weaknesses but as bridges to deeper connections. Teach me to honor my feelings as part of the human experience You designed and to share them in ways that reflect Your love.

---

4   "The Enneacast – Episode #35: Type 5's Enneagram Story w/ Jim Cofield." RelateBetter. Podcast audio, May 5, 2020. https://relatebetter.com/the-enneacast-episode-35-type-5s-enneagram-story-w-jim-cofield/.

Day 8 Reflections:

When have you felt misunderstood or judged due to others' perception that you lack emotion? How can you help them understand and accept your unique emotional processes?

____

____

____

How has maintaining privacy around your emotions and thoughts affected your relationships?

____

____

____

What steps can you take to be more present with your emotions and share them with trusted individuals?

____

____

____

→ Respond

Choose a specific emotion you've experienced and share it with someone you trust today, explaining both the emotion and the situation that prompted it.

Day 9:

Stress Management

And Moses lifted up his hand and struck the rock with his staff twice, and water came out abundantly, and the congregation drank, and their livestock. And the LORD said to Moses and Aaron, "Because you did not believe in me, to uphold me as holy in the eyes of the people of Israel, therefore you shall not bring this assembly into the land that I have given them."

—Numbers 20:11-12

WHAT MAKES YOU FEEL STRESSED OUT? INVESTIGATORS commonly mention being activated by feeling pressure to socialize, being surprised by last-minute requests or obligations, or having people intrude on their privacy. Other stressors include being around people who are "slick" or dishonest, clingy or overly emotional, pull you into their emotional drama, don't respect your expertise, push you to share personal information, break confidentiality, or do incompetent work. Drama or conflict of any kind is particularly challenging for all Fives.

> No pressure, no diamonds.
>
> –Thomas Carlyle[1]

---

1   Iam A. Freeman, *Seeds of Revolution: A Collection of Axioms, Passages and Proverbs, Volume 1* (Bloomington, IN: iUniverse, World Harvest, 2014), 74.

When these things happen, you may be surprised to find yourself "suddenly" at the breaking point, ready to blow up in spectacularly public ways.[2] More than once, the humble-but-stressed-out Moses seemed to throw up his hands, telling God he would rather die than deal with the unfaithful Israelites another moment. While the tantrums often occurred in private, some of Moses' meltdowns took place before the entire nation—like when he struck the rock at Meribah.[3]

When stressed, Fives often retreat into isolation, becoming remote and unreachable. They may neglect self-care, forgetting to eat healthily, exercise, or maintain a tidy environment. This manifests as a racing, restless mind, hyperactivity, impatience and impulsivity, taking on too many projects (without completing others first), or seeking quick fixes to buy time and save resources. Transitioning to the lower side of Type Seven, they may numb themselves with overeating, oversleeping, overspending, or excessive activity, losing their sense of grounding and boundaries.

> Under stress, Fives react rather than respond to life.

The next move Fives make in stress and unhealth is to the low side of Type Eight. Under stress, Fives *react* rather than respond to life, failing to think through the consequences of their behavior. In this space, they become angry, rude, critical, cynical, or condescending.[4] However, there are times when they can discover their power in a healthy manner. If someone has violated boundaries or mistreated them or a loved one, healthy Fives assert themselves and take a stand! Furthermore, when they access the healthy side of Type Seven in stress, they get out of their castle and move toward others, drawing on a unique sense of humor to help them cheer up, becoming more spontaneous and playful, and sharing an optimistic view of the world and the future.[5]

The Good News for Investigators is that there is a way to bend without breaking. There will be times when you come to a breaking point because you feel like you've

---

2   Beth McCord and Jeff McCord, *Becoming Us: Using the Enneagram to Create a Thriving Gospel-Centered Marriage* (Nashville, TN: Morgan James Publishing, 2020).

3   Numbers 20:10-13

4   Cron and Stabile, *The Road Back to You*, 184-185.

5   Wagner, *Nine Lenses on the World*, 325-326.

been spread too thin—like the world is caving in on you. In these moments, you may want to throw in the towel, throw up your hands, and say, "Just leave me alone, people!" But when these things happen, the God who is "merciful and gracious, slow to anger and abounding in steadfast love and faithfulness"[6] will restore you, providing the strength to give people another chance.

God is "long-suffering," meaning He is willing to wait with patience long before giving up on people. Because He has a long fuse, He does not throw a tantrum or run away from us, but is merciful and forbearing. And just as Jesus' life was emptied unjustly on the cross yet reverberated love, you too can pour out grace on even the most intrusive and demanding people in your life—those whom you have chosen to live near and love. God is willing to give you a longer fuse so you can act honorably before all and "uphold [the LORD] as holy in the eyes of the people"[7]—the very thing Moses failed to do at Meribah.

The next time you feel the kettle getting hot, slow down and bring your anxieties to Christ. Resolve to *stay put*, working through conflict with others rather than self-isolating. Ask clarifying questions rather than assuming they are purposefully draining you. Remember, they may not have your sense of boundaries, but God still loves them and wants you to love them.

→ Pray

Father, thank You for sending Your Son to be our example of someone who bent without breaking. Through temptation, opposition, persecution, and even death, He did not throw in the towel. Oh Lord, let the same compassion flow out of me that flowed out of Jesus when He was struck on the cross.

---

6   Psalm 86:15

7   Numbers 20:12

Day 9 Reflections:

What activates your stress most often? What is your usual response?

How can you address your anxiety now to prevent a public meltdown like the one Moses experienced?

Where in your past might you have experienced relational trauma that still needs to be addressed?

→ Respond

Because others may be able to see the warning signs before you do, ask someone to share how they can tell when you are stressed out.

Feeling Misunderstood

He was in the world, and the world was made through him, yet the world did not know him. He came to his own, and his own people did not receive him.

—John 1:10-11

TIM BURTON'S DEEPLY CAPTIVATING FILM, *EDWARD SCISSORHANDS*, revolves around the unique and gentle man, Edward. Created and educated in isolation by an eccentric inventor, Edward is left alone and unfinished, with sharp scissor blades for hands, when the inventor passes away. Living alone in a gothic mansion, he remains hidden away from society until one day, when a kind-hearted, door-to-door saleswoman named Peg discovers Edward. Intrigued by his presence and pitying his loneliness, she brings him home to live with her family.

> It is strange to be known so universally and yet to be so lonely.
>
> —Albert Einstein[1]

Edward's character, like all Investigator Types, must learn how to embrace his own uniqueness while learning to navigate this world full of other people. He must wrestle with a sense of belonging among people who feel everything from love to deep

---

1   Greg Laurie, *Why Believe? Exploring the Honest Questions of Seekers* (Carol Stream, IL: Tyndale House Publishers, 2002), 19.

dislike for him. While he is deeply immersed and content in his own world of creation, sculpting elaborate topiaries for his new neighbors, Edward's struggle to interact with others leads to misunderstandings and further isolation. He grapples with social anxiety and discomfort in new situations, and often feels like an outsider trying to navigate a world that doesn't understand him and his orientation to life.

Fives may feel like misfits or outsiders who find it challenging to blend into society for a few reasons: their intellectual depth can alienate them from others who may not share their level of curiosity or passion for learning. Their preference for substantive conversations over small talk can make it difficult for others to engage with them, so they often find it easier to connect with one or two friends who share their interests. While they may enjoy belonging to a winning debate team, engaging in casual conversations that aren't issue-driven can be difficult. As one Five noted, "I could win arguments but not friends."[2]

While some Fives enjoy competitive sports, most avoid strenuous physical activity whenever possible. Fast-paced environments that don't allow time to strategize or practice at their own pace, along with the pressure to socialize or be enthusiastic, can be draining.

> Fives may feel like misfits or outsiders who find it challenging to blend into society.

Therefore, many Fives choose to spend most of their time on academics or developing their cognitive skills, naturally limiting opportunities to engage socially. This heavy concentration on their inner world might make them appear arrogant or aloof to others, but that is typically a misunderstanding. The great medieval theologian Thomas Aquinas, for example, was called a "dumb ox" by his classmates. However, those hurtful young men had no idea that the quiet boy in their lessons was a humble philosopher who would change the intellectual trajectory of their faith.[3]

Many Fives struggle with social anxiety and feel out of place in groups. Peer interactions can be confusing, awkward, or strained. Their quirky, off-beat, and whimsical sense of humor is drawn to unconventional topics, or is fascinated by

---

2   Calhoun and Loughrige, *Spiritual Rhythms*, 136.

3   Rohr and Ebert, *The Enneagram*, 117.

the absurdities and ironies of life that others may not "get." They easily observe the social cliques forming around them and may find it difficult to fit in with the "cool kids," and often find themselves disliked or at least perceived as odd.

The Good News for Investigators is Jesus knows what it feels like not to be well-received—to feel strange, awkward, and misunderstood in the world *He* created. Not only did He know that prophets are often misunderstood or rejected by those nearest them (Mark 6), but on a deeper level, as the apostle John reported, "He was in the world, and the world was made through him, yet the world did not know him. He came to his own, and his own people did not receive him."[4] Jesus was often the recipient of awkward, dismissive glances because people didn't know what box to put Him in.

When you feel excluded, don't resign yourself to the idea that living in isolation, hidden away from society like Edward, is simply an inevitable part of life. Nor is being misunderstood a sign that something is wrong with you. Just as Peg took Edward in to live with her family in a moving act of compassion, God has brought you into His fold. Others may never fully understand you like He does, and that's a reality you'll have to accept, but God affirms: *You belong.* You weren't meant for a different time or place, but you are called to leave your unique mark on *this* world in ways that only you can.

→ Pray

Father, like Edward, I sometimes feel like a misfit, struggling to find my place in this world. It's hard to embrace my uniqueness when I feel like an outsider, like I don't belong. But I know You understand me in ways no one else can. Even when others don't fully get me, You affirm that I belong. Help me embrace my uniqueness as a gift from You.

---

4 John 1:10-11

Day 10 Reflections:

Recall a time in your past when you felt like a misunderstood misfit or outsider. How did that experience shape your perception of yourself and your place in the world?

Can you recall a time when you genuinely felt a sense of belonging, whether it was in a specific place or with a particular group of people? What made those experiences meaningful to you?

How can you learn to appreciate and celebrate your uniqueness, even in situations where you might feel out of place?

➜ Respond

Discover a new community or group of people who share your interests and values, providing a space where you can genuinely be yourself, and your unique gifts are accepted and appreciated.

Day 11:

Renewable Energy

But they who wait for the LORD *shall renew their strength;*

they shall mount up with wings like eagles; they shall run

and not be weary; they shall walk and not faint.

—Isaiah 40:31

ONE OF THE THINGS I KEEP MY eyes on the most throughout the day is my cell phone battery. I love those first few months with a new phone when I know it won't die no matter how much I use it. But it's the worst when I wake up needing to run out quickly, and I didn't charge my phone overnight.

> The more you lose yourself in something bigger than yourself, the more energy you will have.
>
> –Norman Vincent Peale[1]

This is the game Investigators play every day with their own energy. They are constantly evaluating how much physical and emotional resources it will take to accommodate others' requests. With this mindset, even small suggestions can feel like large demands,

---

1   Darlene Zschech, *The Art of Mentoring: Embracing the Great Generational Transition* (Bloomington, MN: Bethany House Publishers, 2011), 69.

which is why Fives, especially the Self-Preservation subtype, fear being *depleted* of energy—and even life itself—if they stay connected to others.[2] For them, the world places excessive demands while offering meager returns. But this fear of depletion extends beyond energy levels to knowledge and material resources as well, which we'll talk more about in future devotions.

While many of more socially-oriented types forget, relating to people is costly, especially when you wake up in the morning feeling like you already don't have enough resources to survive life's expectations. Why are some Fives tempted to cut conversations short, remain quiet, use non-emotional language, hide out in the office, or tell others no? If you're a Five, the answer is obvious, but if you're reading this because a friend or loved one in your life is a Five, you should know: this tendency to run and hide is in *no way* driven by a lack of love for others, but is a survival tactic to avoid catastrophic depletion. Their "factory default" setting tells them that alone time (and lot's of it!) is essential to recharge, while social time only drains the batteries.

> Being alive is not the same as *living*, and God wants you to live.

But what if the operating manual is wrong?

Let me ask: is the point of having a phone to conserve the battery? While conserving resources will keep you alive, *the point* of life is not simply to just keep existing—it is a means to an end. Being alive is not the same as *living*, and God wants you to *live*—to seek out adventures, make strong connections, create memories, spend money to make money, and give what you have away. God wants you to grab life by the horns rather than hold onto it for dear life.

I know this is easier said than done. But it is both possible and logical if you keep in mind that there is such a thing as *renewable* energy. This kind of energy is never fully depleted, because it is derived from outside sources such as sunlight, wind, and rain. Just as renewable energy continuously replenishes, Fives have a God-given "rechargeable battery" with the capacity to grow in strength from *external* sources. Just as a solar panel can't charge itself but depends on the sun,

---

2   Beatrice Chestnut and Uranio Paes, *The Enneagram Guide to Waking Up: Find Your Path, Face Your Shadow, Discover Your True Self* (Charlottesville, VA: Hampton Roads Publishing, 2021), 127.

Fives must expose themselves to social interactions, learning opportunities, creative pursuits, community involvement, physical exercise, travel, business ventures, and other diverse means of stimulating personal growth.

This, of course, does not mean you must suddenly say yes to everything or that you should not have strong personal boundaries. You are still *you*: solitude and silence will never *not* be important for you. But, by actively engaging with the world and tapping into a few, well-chosen external inputs, you can build and maintain a surplus of energy that never runs out.

The Good News for Investigators is that those "who wait for the LORD shall renew their strength."[3] We see a clear example of this when the Israelites were wandering through the desert for forty years. When the Israelites were depleted and stranded, God caused manna to fall from the sky.[4] Always just enough to keep each person and family thriving another day. In the same way, God will continue to give you a daily measure of physical and emotional energy to sustain you in the wilderness. He's not surprised when famines strike, but as in the days of Joseph, has prepared storehouses of grain for the days or years of hardship ahead. Keep running the race, not solely on the power of solitude, but on the renewable supply of God's grace.

→ Pray

Father, teach me the art of abiding in You, where my strength meets Yours, and I become a conduit for Your love to flow through me. Help me release the fear of depletion and trust in Your abundant supply. In surrendering my perceived scarcity, may I discover the richness of Your provision.

---

3   Isaiah 40:31

4   Exodus 16

Day 11 Reflections:

What signs indicate that your energy is being depleted? How do you typically prevent depletion, and what impact does it have on those around you?

Consider the idea that conserving resources is a means to an end, not the point of life. How does this perspective align or challenge your current approach to managing your time, energy, and resources?

What God-given external inputs or activities could you try or depend on more to become sources of renewal and energy for you?

→ **Respond**

Choose a specific task, project, or activity that you are passionate about and commit to devoting more energy to this endeavor than you initially believe you have.

From Scarcity to Abundance

Or which one of you, if his son asks him for bread, will give him a stone?

Or if he asks for a fish, will give him a serpent? If you then, who are

evil, know how to give good gifts to your children, how much more will

your Father who is in heaven give good things to those who ask him!

—Matthew 7:9-11

ONE OF THE TOP FIVE RICHEST PEOPLE on the planet, Warren Buffet, lives in my hometown of Omaha, Nebraska. He purchased his first home for $31,500 in 1958 and has lived there for over 65 years. Despite his wealth, estimated at over $100 billion, 93-year old Buffet is famously frugal. He only spends $4 for breakfast at McDonalds on his five-minute commute to the office everyday, and he only recently swapped his $20 flip phone for an iPhone.[2]

> Faith in God's abundance frees us to open our hands in generosity.
>
> –Lovett Weems, Jr. and Ann Michel[1]

---

1   Lovett H. Weems Jr. and Ann A. Michel, *Generosity, Stewardship, and Abundance: A Transformational Guide to Church Finance* (Lanham, MD: Rowman & Littlefield Publishers, 2021), 125.

2   Cheyenne DeVon, "Billionaire Warren Buffett Still Lives in the Same Home He Bought for $31,500 More than 60 Years Ago." CNBC, March 4, 2023. https://www.cnbc.com/2023/03/03/warren-buffett-lives-in-the-same-home-he-bought-in-1958.html.

Investigators, like Buffet, are natural minimalists, typically living below their means and saving more than they spend. Healthy Fives are good for the world, showing us how to avoid unnecessary purchases, stay out of debt, and take excellent care of the world's resources. However, when this strength gets exaggerated and veers into unhealth, they can live a Spartan lifestyle that affords themselves (or their loved ones) no luxuries, even taking pride in their asceticism.[3] As they say, "money doesn't grow on trees," but a scarcity mindset is less a sign of frugality than a sign of blindness toward abundance.

Paradoxically, a scarcity mindset can grow as your wealth increases. Whether you are a bum or billionaire, an unhealthy Five can live like an Israelite wandering around the desert, expecting only a limited amount of manna from God each day. But the truth is, we're not living in Egypt anymore—just like Warren Buffet isn't living in the Great Depression anymore. You don't have to settle for McDonald's every day, relying solely on the "manna" of the dollar menu. You can indulge in a steak sometimes if you want.

> A scarcity mindset is less a sign of frugality than a sign of blindness toward abundance.

Notice I said *want* and not *need*. I know you don't *need* a steak to survive, just as you don't *need* a newer car or an updated kitchen. But let me ask: Do you *want* one? The growth path for a Five is to cultivate *wants without guilt*, like a Type Seven. They reflect God's abundance and the joy of new experiences, often reminding people that God owns "the cattle on a thousand hills."[4]

You might be thinking, *Isn't that risky? Won't* wanting *lead to excessive* spending? But that's precisely the point. While God values responsible financial management and avoiding frivolous spending, an excessive trust in financial security can lead us to trusting God less. While having savings for emergencies can be comforting, we shouldn't overlook the importance of enjoying life and meeting the desires of others. Are you sacrificing personal enjoyment and generosity—yours and those who depend on you—for the sake of financial security?

---

3   Riso and Hudson, *Personality Types*, 192.

4   Psalm 50:10

When my wife and I took foster parent training, we learned that a common behavior among foster children is hoarding food in their rooms. If they've lived in scarcity before, they may lack trust in their new foster or adoptive parents, leading them to stockpile food in fear for survival. However, as the children heal and begin to trust again, they realize that if they ask for something, their parents will not only give it to them but replenish it.

Fives need to heed Jesus' words: "If you then, who are evil, know how to give good gifts to your children, how much more will your Father who is in heaven give good things to those who ask him!"[5] Your heavenly Father is not a boss, only giving you what you earn and no more, but a generous Father who desires to lavish blessings on you of both physical and relational value. You don't have to deny yourself new things or experiences: when was the last time you asked Him for a new wardrobe, gadget, dream vacation, or supplies for a new hobby or project? While some of these desires may seem selfish, it's important to remember that God delights in showing His children His world's abundance, wanting them to never worry about having enough.

The Good News for Investigators is that your *wants* are not a problem, nor an inconvenience for the God of abundance. Expand your wishlist today without fear; enrich your life and give as freely as you have received. Believe it or not, financial *security* is not God's highest value for you—*generosity* is. And to be a generous person, you have to let God be generous to you first.

→ Pray

Father, I have cherished Your good gifts. Forgive me when I forget about Your abundant provision and fall into a scarcity mindset. Teach me to boldly ask You for what I need and want, knowing You have more than enough. Help me to balance living frugally with also enjoying the abundance You give.

---

5   Matthew 7:11

Day 12 Reflections:

When was the last time you trusted in God's abundant provision instead of living with a scarcity mindset? What blessings did you receive from that trust?

What wants have you denied yourself because you've convinced yourself you don't need them?

How would your life change if generosity became a higher priority than living frugally?

→ Respond

Identify one way you can spoil yourself. Take action by going out and getting it or taking the necessary steps to make it happen.

Giving Generously

But Jesus said, "They need not go away; you give them something

to eat." They said to him, "We have only five loaves here and

two fish." And he said, "Bring them here to me."

—Matthew 14:16-18

FOR INVESTIGATORS, IT'S OFTEN TEMPTING TO SEE life as a small, zero-sum pie. The fear is always just under the surface that if someone else takes a piece, there will be less for us. This fear is why unhealthy Fives aren't known for being cheerful givers but for being stingy when it comes to their tithe and tips. The God of abundance, though, invites Fives to trust Him—to believe He can make the pie bigger for everyone.

> When we give cheerfully and accept gratefully, everyone is blessed.
>
> —Maya Angelou[1]

Jesus' disciples were once surrounded by over five thousand hungry people in the Judean countryside who wanted a piece of this pie. Not only were they legitimately hungry after spending hours searching for

---

1 "A Quote by Maya Angelou." Goodreads. Accessed June 18, 2024. https://www.goodreads.com/quotes/284542-when-we-give-cheerfully-and-accept-gratefully-everyone-is-blessed.

Jesus, but they also were desperate for the Messiah's limited time and attention. So the disciples came to their Teacher and recommended that He command the crowds to disperse so they could get some food. Due to the distance to the nearest town and the lack of transportation, this plan was more difficult than it sounds, which may be why Jesus had a different idea. He told the disciples, "*You give them something to eat.*"[2]

I can imagine the mix of frustration and panic on the disciples' faces. This is the absolute worst situation for Fives, who try very hard to avoid scenarios where they may be overwhelmed by the needs of others or asked to give more than they have. Being independent and self-sufficient by nature, I'm sure most Fives in this scenario would likely have thought, *Those needy people aren't* my *responsibility! Their lack of planning is not my emergency.*

Additionally, Jesus' command would have been particularly difficult for Fives to accept due to their fear of depletion. Even if they were willing to leave Him alone with the fickle crowds to walk to the nearest town, they knew their collected savings wouldn't be sufficient to provide each person with a bite, let alone a meal. In that moment, the disciples might have perceived Jesus' request to empty their bank account for these conference attendees as impossible, unfair, and unreasonable.

> Abundance most often hides beneath the broken pieces.

But the God who created our abundant world *ex nihilo* (literally "out of nothing")[3] was ready to give them yet another sign that the Divine was among them. After Andrew pointed out a boy who had five loaves and two fish, Jesus took the boy's lunch box and miraculously multiplied it to exponential proportions—so much that every person on that hillside ate their fill, and they had twelve baskets of leftovers![4]

The lesson in this incredible story is that abundance most often hides beneath the broken pieces—that apparent scarcity is simply the thin outer layer to a

---

2   Matthew 14:16

3   Nicholas Bunnin and Jijuan Yu, *The Blackwell Dictionary of Western Philosophy* (Hoboken, NJ: Wiley-Blackwell, 2009), 149.

4   John 6:9-13

much deeper richness. Just as the disciples could feed the large crowd with some scraps, so too can you feed the needy among you today. There is no cause for fear of being overwhelmed with others' needs. Even if it feels like your last piece—a simple word of encouragement, a small gift, or a few minutes of your time—in Christ's hands, it can be blessed, broken, and given away into the sustenance of a hungry world.

The Good News for Investigators is Paul's promise to the Philippian church: "God will supply every need of yours according to his riches in glory in Christ Jesus."[5] Notice it doesn't say "some" or "a few" of our needs, but "*all.*" God's abundance isn't limited by our circumstances or by five thousand hungry people on a hillside. His resources are boundless.

As you go about your day, remember that a scarcity mindset leads us to see the world as zero-sum, as a pie with limited pieces, but an abundance mindset leads us to trust that God can make the pie bigger. Embrace the joy of giving, knowing that every time you do, there will miraculously be more to go around.

→ Pray

Father, help me look at the scraps in my lunch box and see amazing potential. Remind me that the little I have is more than enough for others to feast on Your love. Today, I commit to letting You bless me, break me, and give me away so that I can welcome the needy with Jesus' compassion rather than send them away.

---

5 Philippians 4:19

Day 13 Reflections:

Think back to a moment when you performed a small act of kindness that had a significant impact. Describe the effect it had and how it made you feel.

When was the last time you felt empty-handed, like the disciples in the story? How does Jesus' miracle change your perspective on what God can accomplish through you the next time someone comes to you in need?

What is one action you can take to give more material resources away from an abundant heart? Who or what do you have in mind?

➜ Respond

Practice gratitude by keeping a daily journal of blessings and provisions you receive from God. Take note of both big and small blessings and reflect on how God's abundance is evident in your life.

You and Nicodemus

Jesus answered him, "Truly, truly, I say to you, unless one is

born again he cannot see the kingdom of God." Nicodemus said

to him, "How can a man be born when he is old? Can he enter

a second time into his mother's womb and be born?"

—John 3:3-4

THE BIBLICAL NARRATIVE OF NICODEMUS CARRIES A lot of Investigator themes. Nicodemus belonged to the intellectual-leader class of the Jewish faith—a group of passionate, highly educated religious leaders known as the Pharisees. Like a Five wanting to avoid the crowd, he came to Jesus at night to investigate. A Five's greatest fear is public embarrassment: particularly if it concerns their knowledge. Pastor AJ Sherrill points out, "Fives must be

> Mystery creates wonder and wonder is the basis of man's desire to understand.
>
> —Neil Armstrong[1]

---

1   Dan Davies and Debra McGregor, *Teaching Science Creatively* (Milton Park, Abingdon, United Kingdom: Taylor & Francis, 2011), 66.

permitted three essential ingredients for transformation to occur: information, time, and safety."[2]

While some people are more than ready to follow Jesus after an inspirational worship event, the Investigator type typically requires more information first. They want to ask questions and see the angles, to put the puzzle pieces together. Thus, Nicodemus came to Jesus to find out more (in secret, of course). However, as Sherrill notes, Nicodemus was about to find out that Jesus preferred to teach in parables and paradoxes rather than the clear-cut categories of law to which he was accustomed.[3]

Jesus knew Nicodemus was intelligent and studied, so He moved quickly to get him out of the realm of reason and logic and into *mystery*. Jesus said, "Truly, truly, I say to you, unless one is born again he cannot see the kingdom of God."[4] The idea of being born a second time didn't make rational sense to Nicodomus, and when something doesn't make sense for a Five, it's really hard to accept. Jesus went on to explain that we must be born of water *and* Spirit. Still confused, Nicodemus asked, "How can these things be?"[5] But sensing the growing reluctance in Nicodemus to trust Him, Jesus said, "Are you the teacher of Israel and yet you do not understand these things?"[6]

> You don't have to understand something rationally to marvel at its existence.

This rebuke speaks not just to Nicodemus' refusal to get out of his own way but also serves as an alert for all Fives, highlighting that a wealth of intellectual knowledge falls significantly short of authentic understanding. As the apostle Paul would say, there exist individuals who are "always learning and never able to arrive at a knowledge of the truth."[7] Ouch! But here's the point: accumulating information or mastering something does not necessarily lead to true wisdom.

---

2   AJ Sherrill, *The Enneagram for Spiritual Formation: How Knowing Ourselves Can Make Us More Like Jesus* (Grand Rapids, MI: Brazos Press, a division of Baker Publishing Group, 2020), 98-101.

3   Sherrill, *The Enneagram for Spiritual Formation*, 98-101.

4   John 3:3

5   John 3:9

6   John 3:10

7   2 Timothy 3:7

Spiritual insight calls for *humility* and an openness to acknowledge our gaps in understanding. While we are not asked to check our brains at the door, Jesus teaches that spiritual rebirth is the work of the Spirit within, not the result of human effort or intellectual enlightenment.

Although I'm sure Nicodemus still had many unanswered questions by the time Jesus neared the end of His life, you can tell an impact had been made. When the Pharisees started talking about arresting Jesus, Nicodemus (like a Five moving to Eight in health) assertively stood up for Jesus: "Does our law judge a man without first giving him a hearing and learning what he does?"[8] While his pleas did not move these fearful men bent on Jesus' death, when Fives take action, they can be powerful persuaders who craft airtight cases.

On the day Jesus was "lifted up"[9] and crucified, fulfilling the sign He had promised to Nicodemus as evidence for belief, Nicodemus' knowledge appears to have moved from his head to his heart. He was moved to action, joining Joseph of Arimathea in making preparations to bury Jesus, generously footing the steep bill and bringing a mixture of myrrh and aloes that weighed about a seventy-five pounds to prepare Jesus for burial[10]—the exact amount for the burial of a king in that day.

The Good News for Investigators is you don't have to understand something rationally to marvel at its existence. Quantum Mechanics stands as a prime example—a field where particles behave in ways that defy traditional logic, such as being in two places at once. Though it's beyond our comprehension, the mystery still captivates us. In a similar vein, Jesus introduces Nicodemus to the notion that faith is rooted in wonder and awe, not just understanding. He illuminates the idea that divine mysteries need not be resolved for them to be deeply meaningful. They are not hurdles to be cleared but sacred spaces to meet God. Mysteries don't detract us from our intellectual pursuits; rather, they deepen them. They teach us that the richest experiences, whether in the quantum field or our spiritual journey, often transcend rational explanation.

---

8   John 7:51

9   John 3:14

10   John 19:39

> **→ Pray**
>
> Father, help me embrace Your mysteries with humility, finding beauty in the depths of Your creation and the intricacies of faith that defy easy explanation. Guide me to a deeper faith, where awe and wonder at Your mysteries enrich my walk with You, trusting in Your wisdom over my own.

Day 14 Reflections:

What aspects of Nicodemus' story resonate with yours?

How do you reconcile the desire for logical explanations with the acceptance of mystery in your faith?

Nicodemus eventually moved from questioning to taking action. Where do you need to transition from questioning to taking action?

> **→ Respond**
>
> Practice saying "I don't know" more to foster a sense of wonder in the unexplainable mysteries of God, reminding yourself and others that your value isn't contingent on having all the answers.

Day 15:

The Vice of Avarice

Look at the birds of the air: they neither sow nor reap nor gather into barns,

and yet your heavenly Father feeds them. Are you not of more value than they?

—Matthew 6:26

EBENEZER SCROOGE, THE MISERLY AND COLD-HEARTED CHARACTER of Charles Dickens' *A Christmas Carol*, is greedy, selfish, and lonely—so much so that, to this day, we call people with such qualities a "Scrooge." But through a series of supernatural visits from the ghosts of Christmas Past, Present, and Yet to Come, Scrooge is confronted with the consequences of his actions and shriveled, scarcity-minded heart. These encounters lead him to reflect on his past choices and behavior, ultimately sparking a profound change. By the end of the story, Scrooge experiences a spiritual awakening and becomes more compassionate, generous, and open to community, demonstrating a complete reversal of his former ways.[2]

> Your mind is for having ideas, not holding them.
>
> —David Allen[1]

---

1   "Your mind is for having ideas, not holding them," Goodreads, https://www.goodreads.com/quotes/348103-your-mind-is-for-having-ideas-not-holding-them (accessed April 10, 2024).

2   Mary Jane McKinney, *Grammardog Guide to A Christmas Carol* (N.p.: Grammardog.com LLC, 2004), 25.

Though fictional, Ebenezer Scrooge offers a poignant illustration of the Investigator's journey toward transformation. The Five's natural vice is *avarice*, or extreme greed, and their corresponding fixation is *stinginess*, an unwillingness to share. Avarice is often equated with financial greed, which can manifest as building an excessive savings account and obsessively budgeting, hoarding unneeded and unused possessions while refusing to share with or donate to those in need, and even a refusal to spend money on basic needs or life's small luxuries.

However, the Enneagram's more comprehensive version of avarice includes the hoarding of time, energy, affections, or knowledge. This may manifest as withdrawing from social activities or relationships, withholding emotional energy or vulnerability from your loved ones, collecting information or knowledge without sharing, or sitting on wonderful ideas or projects for long periods of time. In everyday conversations, avarice might look like withholding an answer or solution from someone who you think is unfit or undeserving, moments in which you'll have to use honest self-reflection to determine whether you are being discriminatory or following Jesus' valid command to "not throw your pearls before pigs."[3]

> Your needs are not a problem for God.

While the bright side of the Fives' scarcity mindset is their knack for being frugal and resourceful, the challenge arises when Fives become unable to resist collecting when they feel that their future survival is contingent on holding onto the things they have. They're careful not to waste valuable resources and see value in things and ideas the rest of the world takes for granted. It's no surprise that many Fives are natural collectors, cherishing and even forming emotional attachments to art, albums, tools, cards, comic books, or antiques.

While the ability to notice the value in little things is indeed a gift, a life dominated by avarice may mislead you to feel impoverished, like you never have enough inner-resources to meet life's demands, despite the abundance around you. Fives retreat to their protected mountain hoard because "if they shared themselves, they might lose themselves,"[4] and at their worst, they become Scrooges—jaded

---

3   Matthew 7:6

4   Rohr and Ebert, *The Enneagram*, 124.

and untrusting, lacking the vision to see the never-ending abundance of God's world and people.

The Good News for Investigators is that you are more valuable to God than the birds of the air, who never store up what they have into barns but live each day expecting to get what they need.[5] He invites you to live more like the singing birds, rather than hurried squirrels who are working anxiously for their survival, storing up huge stashes for the winter. Unlike the squirrels, no amount of reserves will ever fully remove your fear of depletion—you will never feel truly safe and secure if dominated by avarice. But *your needs are not a problem for God.* Just as the birds rely on God's provision without worry, let go of your fears today and embrace a more carefree lifestyle, trusting in God's abundant supply. Avarice says, "You don't have enough," but God says, "You have—you *are*—more than enough."

→ Pray

Father, forgive me for the times I have withheld my time, energy, money, or affections out of fear. Help me to release my grip on scarcity and embrace abundance. Teach me to live more like the birds of the air, trusting in Your provision each day, knowing You are supplying all my needs according to Your great riches.

---

5   Matthew 6:26

Day 15 Reflections:

What collections do you find yourself drawn to, and how have these items become emotionally significant to you over time?

How is avarice currently showing up in your life—whether it's holding onto your finances, time, energy, affections, or knowledge? Whom do you typically withhold these things from?

Imagine having unlimited energy and resources at your disposal. You could never, ever, run out of what you need. How do you envision your life and relationships changing in such a scenario?

→ Respond

To counter avarice, take a moment to go through your hard drive, bookshelf, bank account, or a room in your home and identify something that you no longer need but could bless someone else with by giving it away.

The Virtue of Non-Attachment

Indeed, I count everything as loss because of the surpassing worth of knowing Christ Jesus my Lord. For his sake I have suffered the loss of all things and count them as rubbish, in order that I may gain Christ.

—Philippians 3:8

NON-ATTACHMENT IS THE CORE VIRTUE OF INVESTIGATORS. In Buddhism, non-attachment refers to the practice of letting go of the craving for things, ideas, or experiences—releasing control of life and the desire to be fully satisfied here and now. Attachment to these things leads only to suffering, but the goal is to achieve a state of freedom where one can fully engage with life without being overwhelmed by desires or attachments.

> To attain knowledge, add things every day. To attain wisdom, remove things every day.
>
> –Lao Tse[1]

The relationship between non-attachment in Buddhism and the Enneagram version for Fives lies in the concept of *letting go.*

---

1   Chestnut and Paes, *The Enneagram Guide to Waking Up*, 129.

According to Enneagram teachers Chestnut and Paes, Fives need to release their grip on what feels necessary to stay safe and open themselves up to a more natural flow of life; the opposite of the Five's vice of avarice, which is all about holding on and holding back.[2]

In the Christian tradition, the concept of letting go is often expressed as putting off our old desires and attitudes.[3] The apostle Paul, in his letter to the Philippians, states that all worldly possessions and achievements are insignificant compared to the surpassing worth of being in relationship with Christ. He emphasizes that true fulfillment comes from knowing Christ intimately, even if it means sacrificing everything else.[4] The losses are different for every Christ follower and may include material possessions, social status, personal ambitions, relationships, comfort, or security, but for Fives in particular, letting go would include releasing the tendency to withhold time and energy, relinquishing control over their agenda, surrendering their untested ideas and assumptions about how the world works, removing their protective barriers, and shedding the inclination to keep all of their feelings or experiences private.

> Embracing non-attachment involves removing unnecessary barriers so that you can give and receive without any restrictions.

Whereas detachment for the Five is about disconnecting from the body of Christ and the redeemed parts of yourself, non-attachment is about abiding in these things, opening yourself up to receiving them with open arms. Embracing non-attachment involves removing unnecessary barriers so that you can *give and receive* without any restrictions—much like a healthy heart that has cleared all blockages, enabling the free flow of blood throughout the body, bringing restoration and rejuvenation.

---

2   Beatrice Chestnut, *The Complete Enneagram: 27 Paths to Greater Self-Knowledge* (Berkeley, CA: She Writes Press, 2013), 235.

3   See Ephesians 4:22-24.

4   Philippians 3:8

To get the blood flowing again and experience a greater sense of zest in life, Chestnut and Paes offer some ways to cultivate the virtue of non-attachment: First of all, raise your expectation to receive attention, care, and love from those around you—rather than securing those things for yourself—even if some people aren't dependable. Put yourself out there in the world, pursuing and initiating, rather than waiting for God's blessings to magically show up at your house like the Amazon truck. When you do encounter others, engage them with your *heart*, not just your *head*. Let go of the need to demonstrate how much you know and try to become a sponge, soaking in the feelings and insights of others that you could not have arrived at on your own. With humility, hold your worldview and black-and-white categories more loosely; be fully present and create meaningful connections with others in the moment, letting your feelings escape your body now, rather than a few days later.

During the day, prepare yourself for divine interruptions, being ready to receive whatever or whomever God brings, without trying to exert too much control over your schedule. Go with the flow and leave room for more spontaneous requests. Though retreating is much safer, push yourself to be brave and stay with others just a little longer: catch yourself in the act when you are about ready to leave a conversation or social setting and challenge yourself to ask one more question.[5]

The Good News for Investigators is that by gaining Christ, you gain everything you need. Just as the parts of your physical body swiftly work in harmony to aid an injured part, so too will the body of Christ come to meet all your needs when you are empty or hurting. Jesus said, "Whoever abides in me and I in him, he it is that bears much fruit."[6] Abiding in Jesus isn't merely a sentiment found on a coffee cup; it's a daily act of obedience for all Fives to courageously let go of their attachments and become interconnected, interdependent, and inseparable from the life-giving source that is Jesus Himself.

---

5   Chestnut and Paes, *The Enneagram Guide to Waking Up*, 145.

6   John 15:5

> **→ Pray**
>
> Father, I count all my attachments as insignificant compared to the surpassing worth of knowing Your Son, Jesus Christ. Help me to dwell in Your presence with open arms and remove the unnecessary barriers that hinder my ability to freely give and receive. Make me receptive to whatever or whoever You want to bring into my life today.

Day 16 Reflections:

What new insights or clarifications have you gained today about the virtue of non-attachment?

On your spiritual journey so far, what things have you considered as loss compared to knowing Christ? What else might it be time to release?

Which of the suggestions from Chestnut and Paes would you like to work on next to experience a greater sense of rejuvenation in your life?

> **→ Respond**
>
> Commit to being open and receptive to an unplanned conversation or invitation today. Practice being present and allocating more time for it than you are initially comfortable with.

The Office Expert

Then I said to them, "You see the trouble we are in, how Jerusalem

lies in ruins with its gates burned. Come, let us build the wall

of Jerusalem, that we may no longer suffer derision."

—Nehemiah 2:17

SIR ARTHUR CONAN DOYLE'S ICONIC FICTIONAL DETECTIVE, Sherlock Holmes, is celebrated for his exceptional observation skills, analytical prowess, and unconventional methods. His breadth of knowledge and keen intellect allow him to solve cases that baffle the official inspectors of his time. However, without his colleague and friend, Dr. Watson, to model empathy and, yes, to be appropriately impressed by Holmes' abilities, the stories would be far less interesting. Doyle's character serves as an exemplary model for Investigators, particularly as they navigate professional environments. Like Holmes, healthy Fives don't merely indulge their intellect for personal gratification but apply it to real-world challenges. In the right

> I cannot live without brain-work. What else is there to live for?
>
> –Sherlock Holmes[1]

---

1 Cron and Stabile, *The Road Back to You*, 174.

circumstances, they can also be highly collaborative team members, displaying the same kind of beautiful camaraderie seen between Holmes and Watson.

Fives often become the office expert in their fields, using their knowledge to further the team's mission. As masters of observation, they can become brilliant artists or engineers, professors or librarians, computer programmers or psychologists. Whatever they do, their analytical superpower is to drive research, planning, and innovation, and to help their coworkers understand how everything works and fits together. While more assertive types like the spotlight, Fives don't seek affirmation from others or feel a need to be the center of attention or get credit for things. (Holmes constantly told Watson that he did not need to publish their investigative exploits.) While there's nothing wrong with this, some Fives may get passed over for promotions if their bosses view them as too modest or reserved.

Fives excel in fostering an environment characterized by professionalism and are known for their attentive listening skills, thoughtfulness, courtesy, and respect toward others. Because they are self-sufficient and

> You must not sit on your brilliant ideas, but take decisive action.

undramatic, they don't require a lot of attention or supervision. Their insatiable intellectual curiosity and commitment to learning render them invaluable assets to any team. If their expertise and resourcefulness are properly utilized, they will aid their coworkers in accessing and comprehending crucial information for success. Finally, when at ease, they bring warmth, friendliness, and humor to their interactions.[2]

To excel in the workplace, Fives thrive on predictability. They benefit from clear expectations, well-defined deadlines, and having meeting agendas provided in advance. If they know what the demands will be, they can better conserve their time and energy, and if they know what the topics will be, they can show up more competently. Fives also require autonomy: their workplace "hell" is an open floor plan with lots of desks, talkative teammates, meetings that go late, and endless group projects. They need a private space to focus and work independently on an interesting project without interruptions.

---

2 Chestnut, *The 9 Types of Leadership*, 170, 179.

One biblical figure that Fives can learn from is Nehemiah, the fifth century BC Jewish deportee who supervised the rebuilding of Jerusalem. After hearing Jerusalem's walls were broken down and its gates destroyed by fire, he sat and wept for days—praying and fasting. But then, rather than waiting for God to send someone else, Nehemiah realized God wanted him to be the answer to his own prayer. He traveled to Jerusalem, secretly surveyed the rubble, and determined the size and scope of the project before committing to it.[3] Similarly, Fives can take charge, delegate, and put together blueprints like Nehemiah. They can be unstoppable workers, remaining committed for years to a project that others might give up on. However, Fives would benefit from adopting Nehemiah's initiative: He didn't sit on his plans because he didn't have enough information. Rather, he took a risk, knowing *the worst action is to take no action.*

The Good News for Investigators is that Nehemiah, a lowly cupbearer, got permission to rebuild David's City from the king of his captor, Artaxerxes.[4] Though his ambitious engineering plan may have seemed too risky, God opened a door that would change the Jewish nation forever. Because Nehemiah didn't just "think about it" but also got to work, he paved the way for the Messiah's triumphal entry into Jerusalem centuries later. Like Nehemiah, God will use you to do things that seem impossible—but you must not sit on your brilliant ideas, but take decisive action. Like Nehemiah, others—perhaps even those yet to be born—are counting on your leadership.

→ Pray

Father, thank You for giving me incredible gifts and abilities. Help me to keep praying big, bold prayers as I dream about my ideas coming to fruition. I know if I ask anything in Your name, You'll make it happen.[5] Like Nehemiah, I will trust in Your guidance and take decisive action to fulfill Your plans for my life.

---

3   Nehemiah 1:3–2:8

4   Nehemiah 1:11, 2:8

5   John 16:23

Day 17 Reflections:

Which of the workplace strengths do you see most in yourself? Please explain.

____

____

____

____

What do you need in your workplace to thrive? Have you effectively communicated these needs to your boss?

____

____

____

____

How can you strike a balance between thorough research and planning while also prioritizing action?

____

____

____

____

➜ Respond

Write down a seemingly impossible project you would like your team to accomplish if you, like Nehemiah, know God's hand is on you. Then rally the "Watsons" in your life to assist you in accomplishing it.

Surviving the Workplace

Fear not, for I am with you; be not dismayed, for I am your God; I will strengthen you, I will help you, I will uphold you with my righteous right hand.

—Isaiah 41:10

INVESTIGATORS CAN FACE SIGNIFICANT CHALLENGES IN THE workplace, especially when *other* people are involved. The environment can often be fast-paced and demanding, leaving insufficient time to complete work to their exacting specifications—which is also why they find others' sloppy work so frustrating. Some of the Five's work pet peeves include being interrupted in the middle of a project, being tasked with last-minute assignments or working with incompetent or disorganized leaders, and being expected by their colleagues to discuss personal matters or emotions.[2] Fives can be desperate to keep their

> You will not have a meaningful life without work, but you cannot say that your work is the meaning of your life.
>
> –Timothy Keller[1]

---

1   Timothy Keller and Katherine Leary Alsdorf, *Every Good Endeavor: Connecting Your Work to God's Work* (New York: Penguin Books, 2016), 40.

2   Chestnut, *The 9 Types of Leadership*, 177.

boundaries in place, and prefer clearly defined roles so they don't get sucked into someone else's responsibilities—or worse, their personal lives! They also expect everyone to strictly adhere to the designated time limit for meetings, or to keep personal discussion to a minimum while working. If "Chatty Cathy" is still going long after it's time to move on to the next task, they can feel a physical discomfort.

As we discussed yesterday, Fives bring many strengths to the workplace, yet like everyone else, they can face challenges when their strengths are overused. It's crucial to remain mindful of the transition from healthy autonomy to potentially isolating oneself. Others *will* take notice if you retreat into your office, shut the door, and become inaccessible—particularly if this happens during times others are socializing. Remember, the workplace is filled with *human beings*, not cogs in a machine. If there's one thing the critically-acclaimed comedy series *The Office* shows, it's that people—yes, even those people who seem to be distractions from your work—are the real thing that makes labor seem less laborious. Become more accessible and willing to discuss personal stories or non-work-related topics and share the non-work topics you find stimulating. Aim to accept more invitations to engage in casual conversations in the break room, join colleagues for lunch, or linger to share in celebrating someone's birthday with cake and ice cream.

> **Aim to be more personal than utilitarian.**

Aim to be more personal than utilitarian. Don't allow your rational mind, which is undoubtedly a strength, to become a hindrance by dismissing feelings in the workplace, lowering the temperature by what others perceive as coldness. Remember the wisdom of the apostle Paul's encouragement to "rejoice with those who rejoice, weep with those who weep."[3] Yes, even at work. Embracing emotions will also allow you to form deeper friendships, and research suggests that having a best friend at work significantly impacts job satisfaction.[4]

Finally, strive to cultivate greater flexibility. Your grounded and focused nature may make it difficult to shift gears quickly, but adaptability is crucial for survival. Embrace change and spontaneity as allies rather than threats, welcoming them

---

3   Romans 12:15

4   Marcus Buckingham and Curt Coffman, *First, Break All the Rules: What the World's Greatest Managers Do Differently* (Washington, DC: Gallup Press, 2014), 35.

when they appear. Be open to adjusting your conceptual frameworks, mental models, or systems as needed, and remember that sometimes it's necessary to entirely let go of old ways to embrace new ideas or approaches.

The Good News for Investigators is that God is with you not just on Sundays but on Mondays and every day of the week. He promises to strengthen you when you feel weakened by the demands of working for your daily bread. Jesus understands the unique struggles you encounter in the workplace—when others totally disregard your expertise, rudely overstep your boundaries, or misunderstand your intentions. It's inevitable that others will misconstrue moments when you are deep in thought as indifference or arrogance. Jesus empathizes with the frustration you feel in these moments, so find strength and reassurance in His presence as you navigate the complexities of the workplace, especially in interactions with others.

→ Pray

Father, help me navigate the demands and complexities of the workplace with wisdom. Give me patience and grace when interruptions and last-minute tasks arise. Teach me to create space to empathize with the joys and struggles of others. Thank You for understanding my frustrations and upholding me every step of the way.

Day 18 Reflections:

What workplace situations trigger the most frustration or discomfort for you? How do you usually handle these situations when they arise?

When has your need for autonomy, independence, boundaries, or privacy negatively impacted your team dynamics? What did you learn from that experience?

How can you "humanize" your work? In other words, what is one step you can take to cultivate personal connections and prioritize the interpersonal dynamics of your job?

→ Respond

To prevent misunderstandings, consider having a discussion with your manager or team members about your need for downtime to recharge, the possibility of a quieter workspace for improved focus, advanced notice for requests, and the importance of adhering to meeting schedules.

Thinking Your Feelings

Then Moses stretched out his hand over the sea, and the LORD drove the sea back by a strong east wind all night and made the sea dry land, and the waters were divided. And the people of Israel went into the midst of the sea on dry ground, the waters being a wall to them on their right hand and on their left.

—Exodus 14:21-22

IN THE UNIVERSE OF STAR TREK, FEW characters exemplify the journey from strict rationalism towards embracing the complexity of emotions as vividly as Spock. As a Vulcan, Spock initially prides himself on his logical, unemotional demeanor, viewing emotions as a weakness to be overcome. He shares, "May I say that I have not thoroughly enjoyed serving with Humans? I find their illogic and foolish emotions a constant irritant."[2] However, as the series

> We cannot selectively numb emotions. When we numb the painful emotions, we also numb the positive emotions.
>
> –Brené Brown[1]

---

1   Brené Brown, *The Gifts of Imperfection: Let Go of Who You Think You're Supposed to Be and Embrace Who You Are* (Center City, MN: Hazelden Publishing, 2010), 70.

2   "'Star Trek' Day of the Dove." IMDb. Accessed June 18, 2024. https://www.imdb.com/title/tt0708427/characters/nm0001150.

unfolds, Spock's interactions with his human counterparts, especially Captain Kirk and Dr. McCoy, gradually open his eyes to the value and necessity of emotions.

Spock's transformation is vital for the Investigator to observe. For Fives, Like Spock, "emotions are not on tap" as my friend and Enneagram author Jesse Eubanks says. Rather, Fives have to "think their way to their feelings."[3] If you ask a Five what they feel, they will tell you what they think.[4]

One of the go-to defense mechanisms of the Five is *isolation*, which is defined by psychologist Nancy McWilliams as the separation of *feeling* from *knowing* to avoid painful emotions.[5] This mechanism can sometimes be very useful, particularly in high-stress jobs where a person's actions could have fatal consequences. For example, doctors, law enforcement officers, soldiers, and judges need to distance themselves from emotions that could be detrimental to their jobs and others' lives. Additionally, emotions are often a source of conflict. The wise sage, King Solomon, put it this way: "A hot-tempered man stirs up strife, but he who is slow to anger quiets contention."[6] That is why healthy Fives, who are neither ruled nor easily led astray by emotions, are so good to have in our lives!

> An emotionless life is an impoverished life.

Yet there is always another side to the story. While it's true that emotions can become barriers to well-being (yours and others'), it is equally true that an emotionless life is an impoverished life. Just imagine how impoverished our spiritual tradition would be without the Psalms, or Ecclesiastes, or the apostle Paul's raw love, grief, and even anger toward the early churches. While they can seem a nuisance, I encourage you to value your emotions more highly, recognizing that they're not just disturbances but *crucial* to our humanity. Emotions like joy, sadness, anger, fear, and disgust are core to our being. When a Five starts cutting these off, they end up amputating the parts of themselves that make them beautiful and whole.

---

3   Cron and Stabile, *The Road Back to You*, 176.

4   Sherrill, *The Enneagram for Spiritual Formation*, 52.

5   Chestnut, *The Complete Enneagram*, 233-234.

6   Proverbs 15:18

Emotions are crucial for personal and spiritual growth, and bypassing them may cause you to miss out on important developmental stages. Simply filling the "potholes" left by the pressures of life with more analytical thinking will cause you to fall short of real transformation. Emotions are essential for connecting with others and fostering communal bonding. Moreover, our emotions also serve a critical role in the process of individual and group memory formation: they help us solve problems better and let us know when something needs fixing or changing or when we should be rewarded. In other words, emotions can make us *more* fulfilled and even more competent in our work.

The Good News for Investigators is that you can navigate deep emotional waters without drowning in them. Morgan Harper Nichols, an artist and author of *Forty Days on Being a Five*, likens emotions to the walls of the Red Sea that the Israelites followed Moses through. With tremendous courage, Nichols walks the path every day, fearing that her emotions could come crashing down at any moment and engulf her.[7]

That trepidation of being consumed by your emotions is undoubtedly real! Yet, it's crucial to realize that the path to where God intends for you lies through the path of confronting these emotions head-on, walking between the towering, fearful waters, not sidestepping them. Take solace in knowing that as you delve into the depths of your feelings—even those that seem most daunting—you are not alone but are accompanied by the very One who has the power over the sea and guides you through safely.

→ Pray

Father, help me to embrace both logic and emotion, recognizing them as gifts that deepen my humanity and connection to myself and others. As I face my fears and navigate the depths of my feelings, remind me that I am never alone. Thank You for being my constant companion, the One who commands the seas and calms the storms within my heart.

---

7   Morgan Harper Nichols, *Forty Days on Being a Five* (Downers Grove, IL: InterVarsity Press, 2021), Day 21.

Day 19 Reflections:

What is your relationship to emotions? Have you made an accidental virtue out of keeping them at bay? Explain.

____

____

____

____

Where can you identify moments when you've detached from your emotions and replaced them with thinking to maintain control?

____

____

____

____

How would embracing emotions as vital for personal and spiritual growth shift your response to emotionally charged situations?

____

____

____

____

→ Respond

Even if it's uncomfortable to see your emotions in writing, begin a "Feeling Journal." Record your emotions as they happen, focusing on those you typically ignore.

Wearing Your Heart

If I speak in the tongues of men and of angels, but have

not love, I am a noisy gong or a clanging cymbal.

—1 Corinthians 13:1

IMAGINE STEPPING INTO A GRAND HALL AND hearing those unmistakable notes of an orchestra warming up. Surrounded by the hushed anticipation of eager listeners, you take your seat and find a neatly folded sheet of music waiting for you. Looking at the intricate notes and symbols sprawled across the page, you realize this is the score for the pieces you are about to hear. Technically, in that moment, you possess the essence of the music—the melodies, and harmonies, the tempo and dynamic markings—but while in your hand, it remains inert, devoid of life and vibrancy until it's brought to life by the skilled hands of the musicians.

> The problem is you love your family in your heart. But you don't love them in your schedule. And they can't see your heart.
>
> –Andy Stanley[1]

---

1   Andy Stanley, *When Work and Family Collide: Keeping Your Job from Cheating Your Family* (New York City: Crown Publishing Group, 2011), 44.

Understanding the emotions of Investigators can resemble receiving sheet music without hearing the tune: they may catalog their feelings meticulously, neatly arranging them like a well-organized score, but for others, even those skilled at reading them, it is still a silent symphony.

Healthy Fives communicate with clarity and precision, prioritizing listening before speaking, and have an economical approach to their words. They seek to say exactly what they mean, and when they succeed, they can be some of the best conversationalists on the Enneagram! However, the most consistent feedback from loved ones is that average Fives play their cards too close to the vest, offering non-committal responses that don't require any action or sharing on their part: agreeable noises like "Hmmm" and "Ohhh" or non-committal replies like "That's interesting."[2] Unhealthy Fives hoard their thoughts and feelings, giving others the impression they are disinterested or disengaged and only sharing a fraction of what others share with them. When friends ask, "Why didn't you tell me that before?" Fives may, with confusion on their face, respond, "Because you never asked." When loved ones ask why there hasn't been a lot of verbal affirmation, Fives may say, "Well, I already told you I loved you on your birthday."

> When you let your guard down and show your lighthearted side, it's incredibly heartwarming.

Even if you don't feel the *need* to wear your heart on your sleeve, it's always a good reminder that relationships thrive on *mutuality*. Listening is a great asset of yours, but lasting relationships are built on both parties being vulnerable, so if you never share authentic emotions, others won't be able to mirror them back supportively; they won't be able to empathize with you if you don't give them something to empathize with.[3]

A good practice is to try to reach out to others before they reach out to you. Fives are notorious for befriending people who make the first move, so try to beat others to the punch, letting them know you are thinking of them. Use these opportunities of chosen quality time to practice getting in touch with your

---

2   Calhoun and Loughrige, *Spiritual Rhythms*, 142.

3   Wagner, *Nine Lenses on the World*, 311.

feelings by paying attention to your bodily sensations in real time. It's more advantageous to your relationships if you allow joy and grief to come up in the present rather than a few days later when you're having coffee alone. You can also work on your nonverbals in these interactions: maintaining eye contact, smiling more, and yes, even leaning in for a hug sometimes (no matter how awkward it feels). When you let your guard down and show your lighthearted side, it's incredibly heartwarming. Allowing yourself to be more silly makes you even more relatable and lovable.

The Good News for Investigators is that we worship a King who could have communicated with impressive displays of profound knowledge speaking "in the tongues of men and of angels"[4] but instead chose the path of vulnerability. He embodied the apostle Paul's reminder in 1 Corinthians 13:1 that even the most articulate speech is meaningless without love. You may pride yourself on clear, precise, or detailed thought and communication. Yet, if these attributes are not grounded in physicalized, localized love, they risk becoming devoid of the empathy and understanding that genuine connection demands. Listen to Paul's challenge to recognize the transformative power of love in your communication: when you wear your heart on your sleeve, your words will become more than musical notes on a page and will instead transform into a symphony that warms the hearts of others.

→ Pray

Father, I'm like a sheet of music in Your hands—full of intricate notes waiting to be heard. Help me to embrace vulnerability. Show me the beauty in reaching out to others and being more openhearted. Remind me of Your example to choose expressive love over solitary stoicism. May my words to others become a symphony of warmth and connection.

---

4   1 Corinthians 13:1

Day 20 Reflections:

How do you find yourself holding back or playing it safe in your communication style? Can you recall any specific instances where you've received feedback about this (even if others didn't know how to express these feelings of disconnection)?

Think back to a moment when you chose to let your guard down. What fears were hindering you, and what happened when you decided to step out of your comfort zone?

What is a small step you can take to wear your heart on your sleeve more, incorporating more warmth into both your verbal and nonverbal communication?

➤ **Respond**

Practice vulnerability by sharing with someone close to you a thought or feeling that's still percolating, taking the risk to do so regardless of how you think they'll respond.

Boundaries or Fences

My refuge and my fortress, my God, in whom I trust.

—Psalm 91:2

IN THE PHYSICAL WORLD, BACKYARD FENCES ARE helpful because they define where our property ends and another's begins. Similarly, God created boundaries to be fences for our souls, keeping us from becoming doormats.[2] When you say no to good people or great opportunities, others may perceive it as selfish; however, Dr. Henry Cloud clarifies that boundaries are not about selfishness but *stewardship*.[3] Setting boundaries protects the limited time and resources God has given you to leverage for His glory. However, there is a warning for Fives in this principle of healthy separation: boundaries should never become impenetrable fences.

> I will not let anyone walk through my mind with their dirty feet.
>
> —Gandhi[1]

---

1   "I will not let anyone walk through my mind with their dirty feet," Goodreads, https://www.goodreads.com/quotes/2450-i-will-not-let-anyone-walk-through-my-mind-with (accessed April 23, 2024).

2   "What Are Healthy Boundaries?" *Boundaries Books*, accessed November 16, 2020, https://www.boundariesbooks.com/pages/what-are-healthy-boundaries.

3   "Am I Being Selfish When I Set Boundaries?" *Boundaries Books*, accessed November 16, 2020, https://www.boundariesbooks.com/blogs/boundaries-blog/am-i-being-selfish-when-i-set-boundaries.

Consider the mid-twentieth century: American culture saw the decline of the front porch as the gathering space for neighbors, replaced by backyard patios hidden by privacy fences. While front porches had traditionally served as hubs of social interaction and connection, the allure of private outdoor spaces enticed homeowners to retreat into secluded sanctuaries within their own property, a transition which not only altered the physical appearance of neighborhoods but also contributed to a reshaping of the way Americans related to one another.[4]

Just as the culture shifted from spending time on the open front porch to the hidden backyard, Investigators can easily make this transition as well—literally or metaphorically. Most Enneagram types want some amount of private space, but Fives *need* it. They think social-types will ask too many personal questions, introspective-types will make them take another personality test, aggressive-types will drain their energy, bossy-types will "should" on them with more to-dos, and needy-types will take more than they give. That's why every Five needs a t-shirt that says, "It's too peopley outside."

There must be a balance between creating open borders to your life and impenetrable fences—a space for *healthy boundaries*. We can summarize some of the key differences below:

• *Healthy boundaries are flexible while fences are inflexible.* This could look like choosing to expand your social circle when someone intrigues you rather than remaining with your small, well-known group.

• *Healthy boundaries are open to negotiation, but fences are not.* This could look like adjusting plans based on someone else's availability instead of insisting on your own timetable.

• *Healthy boundaries encourage healthy communication while fences cut it off entirely.* This could look like openly discussing hurts or needs in conflict instead of retreating and remaining unreachable.

---

4   Andres Duany, Elizabeth Plater-Zyberk, and Jeff Speck, *Suburban Nation: The Rise of Sprawl and the Decline of the American Dream* (New York: Farrar, Straus and Giroux, 2000).

- *Healthy boundaries foster interdependence, whereas fences reinforce unhealthy independence (or codependence with the one person you have allowed in).* This could look like having an on-call or open-door policy, leaving your phone on or door open during certain times of the day to provide support for others.

- *Healthy boundaries promote transparency while fences promote secrecy.* This could look like holding regular team meetings to communicate and allow feedback, as opposed to a leader withholding information and making decisions behind closed doors.

Privacy, when taken to an extreme by unhealthy Fives, can become a prison: a space that once felt comfortable and safe can morph into one where others give up knocking on your door or sending you texts. While a strategy of hiding can be effective when faced with genuine threats, prolonged isolation can make it harder for others to reach out to you when you need them to, so embrace both your front porch and private backyard, balancing rejuvenating solitude with human connection.[5]

The Good News for Investigators is you were not created to be a prisoner to the expectations of others, to the detriment of your own life. When the psalmist felt vulnerable and overwhelmed by others, he cried out, "My refuge and my fortress, my God, in whom I trust."[6] Take a hold of these words today and look to Jesus who is your fortified hiding place, the One who will protect you on all sides. Because He protects you, you don't need to hide away in insecure obscurity and can ease up on maintaining your fences to live with courageous transparency, occasionally welcoming those whom God places on your front porch.

---

5   Helen Palmer, *The Enneagram in Love and Work: Understanding Your Intimate and Business Relationships* (New York, NY: HarperOne, 2010), 134-135.

6   Psalm 91:2

> **→ Pray**
>
> Father, help me set healthy boundaries without building impenetrable fences. May I balance solitude and community, knowing when to retreat and when to open up. Guide me to have more flexible boundaries that encourage communication and transparency. In moments of vulnerability, be my refuge and protector.

Day 21 Reflections:

What are some healthy boundaries you've established?

Where have these boundaries potentially become rigid fences? Are there areas where you might be excessively enforcing or protecting your boundaries? Explain.

How can you create more opportunities to really connect with people without giving up your alone time?

> **→ Respond**
>
> When you're feeling drained in a group setting, practice gracefully excusing yourself instead of practicing the Five's trademark "Irish Exit" and silently withdrawing. Consider saying, "I just wanted to let you know I'm heading out. Thank you for … ."[7]

---

7 Calhoun and Loughrige, *Spiritual Rhythms*, 145-146.

Navigating Grief

He was despised and rejected by men, a man of sorrows and

acquainted with grief; and as one from whom men hide their

faces he was despised, and we esteemed him not.

—Isaiah 53:3

FOLLOWING THE DEATH OF HIS WIFE IN 1960, C.S. Lewis wrote a deeply personal reflection called *A Grief Observed*. This intensely raw and honest exploration of Lewis' emotions, doubts, and struggles as he grapples with the profound loss of his beloved wife highlights what happens when a great analytical thinker is suddenly swept up in the waves of grief. I don't know if C.S. Lewis was a Five, but the title is certainly representative of a Five. I was fascinated to learn that in Five-like fashion, Lewis wanted to express his grief in anonymity, publishing under the pseudonym N.W. Clerk. He remained anonymous until the printing of the third edition.[2]

> No one ever told me that grief felt so like fear.
>
> –C.S. Lewis[1]

---

1   C.S. Lewis, *A Grief Observed* (United Kingdom: Faber & Faber, 2012), 3.

2   Walter Hooper, *C.S. Lewis: A Companion and Guide* (San Francisco: HarperCollins, 1996), 196.

In the book, Lewis describes the intense and overwhelming nature of grief, likening it to a physical weight that crushes you. He expresses how, when grief comes, it doesn't just knock politely on your door but kicks it down. Grief can consume every aspect of life, leaving little room for anything else, which is why Enneagram authors Liz Carver and Josh Green teach that grief and loss are the Five's *reckoning*: a humbling encounter that forces you to finally deal with the unpleasant emotions suppressed by unconscious compulsions such as rationalization or compartmentalization.[3]

Beatrice Chestnut goes on to explain why grief is so hard for this type: "Because Fives do not live in their emotions, they may be more vulnerable to the effects of emotional pain; they have not built up a tolerance for or a comfort with their emotions and so may not know how to deal with painful feelings. In light of this, Fives may have less ability to feel and weather difficult emotions."[4]

> God won't allow grief to crush you but will use it to craft a more tender version of you.

How do average Investigators respond to grief when it comes knocking? One strategy is withdrawal. I've witnessed Fives distance themselves from loved ones who are sick or dying (some even skip funerals). However, it's not typically due to a lack of empathy, but as a survival tactic. Another way to keep the pain at bay is by compartmentalizing grief. During a painful or traumatic event, Fives tend to separate the facts of what's happening from the intense emotions, which is why their descriptions of the event to therapists or friends are often presented in such a detached way that others may think it happened to someone else, creating a kind of "amnesia" that causes them to lose touch with the weight or impact of the event.[5]

Finally, thinking often becomes a substitute for, not a complement to, feelings in their grief. I once heard a Five say that while he wants to cry, he can't because he feels like he needs to get answers first. That's why the temptation to pull back is

---

3   Liz Carver and Josh Green, *What's Your Enneatype?: Understanding the Nine Personality Types for Personal Growth and Strengthened Relationships* (Beverly, MA: Fair Winds Press, an imprint of The Quarto Group, 2020), 101.

4   Chestnut, *The Complete Enneagram*, 241.

5   Claudio Naranjo, *Character and Neurosis*, 103.

always present when Fives get hit with something beyond their control, hoping to observe the situation from a safe distance until it all makes sense. However, the grim reality is that grief never truly makes sense.

The Good News for Investigators is that God won't allow grief to crush you but will use it to craft a more tender version of you.[6] If you don't avoid grief's unavoidable knock but courageously allow it in and give it a seat at the table, you'll find that it is a teacher, not a grim reaper; the beginning of a process, rather than the end of you. The writer of Ecclesiastes affirms that God has ordained for us "a time to weep, and a time to laugh; a time to mourn, and a time to dance,"[7] and never forget Jesus was called "a man of sorrows and acquainted with grief."[8]

How acquainted are you with grief? Like C.S. Lewis, have you set aside a season to mourn a tragedy or loss? If you learn to hold space for your emotions rather than bypassing them with mental shortcuts, it may not immediately resolve the dissonance, but it can guide you toward a peace that surpasses explanation. Grief can shape you into someone more like the Man of Sorrows, allowing you to be the empathetic friend we need when we go through loss or heartache.[9]

→ Pray

Father, give me the courage to grieve and lament, knowing it is a necessary part of healing and growth. Help me navigate the depths of my emotions rather than bypassing them with mental shortcuts, and empower me to draw close to others in their times of sorrow rather than pulling away in fear.

---

6 Carver and Green, *What's Your Enneatype?* 101.

7 Ecclesiastes 3:4

8 Isaiah 53:3

9 Philippians 4:7

Day 22 Reflections:

Reflect on a time when you experienced grief or loss. Did you find yourself withdrawing or compartmentalizing your feelings, or did you allow yourself to fully experience them?

What are some healthy ways and spaces you can process grief and allow yourself to experience the emotions that come with it?

Who do you know that is grieving right now? How can you support them as they navigate through loss or heartache?

→ **Respond**

Think about a painful experience, and then write a prayer of lament using Psalm 22 as a guide. Express your unvarnished grief over the loss of a loved one, personal failure or disappointments, unfulfilled dreams, childhood experiences, or social injustice.

Day 23:

Embodied

Then the LORD God formed the man of dust from the ground and breathed

into his nostrils the breath of life, and the man became a living creature.

—Genesis 2:7

INVESTIGATORS MAY HAVE SOME OF THE STRONGEST minds of any type, but this often is accompanied by an underdeveloped sense of bodily awareness.[2] They may have grown up believing the mind to be a sanctuary—a safe and dependable refuge in contrast to their bodies, which feel more vulnerable, unreliable, or even useless.[3] It can be so easy for Fives to become trapped in their mind, numbing themselves to their body and the outside world. If the body is neglected altogether, unhealthy Fives will eventually run into problems with their physical health along with emotional and spiritual side effects.

> The body is not a prison to escape from, but a temple in which God already dwells.
>
> –Henri Nouwen[1]

---

1   Henri J. M. Nouwen, *The Road to Daybreak: A Spiritual Journey* (United Kingdom: Crown Publishing Group, 1990), 163.

2   Cron, *The Story of You,* 159.

3   Riso and Hudson, *The Wisdom of the Enneagram,* 229.

Plotinus, founder of the third century philosophical system Neoplatonism, taught that true happiness and knowledge were found in *transcending* the material world, particularly where the "inferior" physical body was concerned. In his biography of Plotinus, Porphyry described his teacher as "a man who is ashamed of being in a body."[4]

Gnosticism, a religious movement in the early Christian era, took it one step further and said that the material world and the body were inherently evil or corrupt—not *fallen* but made of pre-corrupted material which could never be saved and so must be transcended and eventually abandoned.[5]

In contrast to this dualistic way of thinking, the term *embodiment* emphasizes the interconnectedness of our mind and body. It describes the body not as an impediment to understanding but as fundamental for our thinking and reasoning. Far from diminishing the value of intellectual or spiritual pursuits, embodiment suggests these are inherently tied to our physical nature and cannot be fully understood or achieved apart from it.

> Becoming embodied helps Fives feel alive, sparking greater motivation, self-confidence, and assertiveness.

According to Enneagram teaching, healthy Fives move toward Type Eight—part of what is known as the Enneagram's "gut triad"—on their path of growth. While there are one hundred billion neurons in the human brain, there are also five hundred million in the gut: perhaps it's no wonder that physical ailments may arise if we routinely ignore and devalue them![6] Becoming embodied helps Fives feel alive, sparking greater motivation, self-confidence, and assertiveness. This shift encourages them to quiet their minds and become more attuned to their physical sensations, recognizing the body as a valuable source of insight.

---

4   Rohr and Ebert, *The Enneagram*, 117.

5   The Greek word gnōsis means "knowledge" and expresses this amorphous tradition's belief that in order to be saved, we must literally become "mind over matter." Blue Letter Bible, https://www.blueletterbible.org/lexicon/g1108/kjv/tr/0-1/ (accessed May 2, 2024).

6   To start learning more about the gut-brain connection, especially their connection to the polyvagal system, begin here: https://www.healthline.com/nutrition/gut-brain-connection#:~:text=There%20are%20approximately%20100%20billion,connecting%20your%20gut%20and%20brain.

They begin to trust their "gut" intuition, which enables them to engage more effectively in the world.

As an action step, consider participating in activities like yoga, martial arts, running, biking, swimming, athletics, or a daily workout routine to enhance your connection with your body. Other activities could include gardening, painting, sewing, home renovating, or dancing—even, or maybe *especially*, if it feels awkward! To maintain your body's health, create a meal plan with nutritious foods, establish a bedtime to ensure sufficient rest, or schedule that health check-up you've been postponing.

To sweeten the deal, recent studies have shown that physical exercise can boost that brain power Fives care so much about by increasing the production of certain proteins that help brain cells grow and learn. Exercise also changes the brain's structure, making areas important for thinking and memory larger and more active. Moreover, staying active can elevate your mood and diminish anxiety and depression.[7] While the advice to exercise might seem universal, as a Type Five, it's particularly beneficial for you to take this guidance to heart: embracing exercise as a key area for growth can bring about swift and significant improvements.

The Good News for Investigators is that Scripture celebrates the creation of our physical bodies, which are meticulously fashioned by God Himself. Far from being simple containers, the Genesis account of humanity's creation reveals that our bodies are the masterful creation of the Divine brought to life with His very breath. This reminds us of the importance and intentionality of our physical existence. The apostle Paul also assures us that upon death, it's not solely our spirit that will be resurrected, but our bodies too.[8] Our bodies are temples of the Holy Spirit,[9] given to us to care for wisely and lovingly. To see our bodies as anything other than a precious gift is to miss the deliberate and loving craftsmanship with which God made us. So, today, let's honor our bodies as the gifts they are, by listening to their needs, nourishing them well, staying active, and attuning ourselves to their innate wisdom.

---

7 Felice Festa, Silvia Medori, and Monica Macrì. "Move Your Body, Boost Your Brain: The Positive Impact of Physical Activity on Cognition across All Age Groups." *Biomedicines*. Accessed June 18, 2024. https://pubmed.ncbi.nlm.nih. gov/37371860/.

8 1 Corinthians 15:42-44

9 1 Corinthians 6:19-20

> **→ Pray**
>
> Father, thank You for the incredible gift of my body. Guide me to never see it as less important than my mind. Help me to fully embrace my entire being, understanding the profound link between body and spirit. GIve me the discipline to partake in physical activities that awaken my sense of vitality, and let me honor You by taking care of my physical self.

Day 23 Reflections:

Why do you often prioritize intellectual or spiritual activities over physical ones? What false beliefs do you have to overcome?

____

____

____

Reflect on a moment when being deeply connected to your body's sensations guided you to a wiser choice or enhanced your mental or emotional well-being. What lessons did you gain from that experience?

____

____

____

How can you develop a more attentive listening practice to your body's cues and signals on a daily basis?

____

____

____

> **→ Respond**
>
> Identify one physical activity you've never tried but are curious about. How can committing to this activity for a month help you to become more happy and healthy?

Worship with Your Body

You shall love the LORD your God with all your heart

and with all your soul and with all your might.

—Deuteronomy 6:5

IN MIDDLE SCHOOL, MY FATHER TOOK ME to a large worship event in a stadium. When the music started and the large choir began singing, I felt tears welling up in my eyes as the music flowed from voices into my heart, but in that moment I used every ounce of strength I had to stop the tears from coming. Especially when worshiping publicly, I didn't want others to see me showing deep emotion.

> The most valuable thing the Psalms do for me is to express the same delight in God which made David dance.
>
> –C.S. Lewis[1]

I felt chained to appearances, wanting so badly to lift my hands but feeling unable to do so. Have you ever wanted to express yourself, but feared what would happen if you tried to "get loose" in your body?

After many years of taking baby steps, I now raise my hands freely during musical worship. Gone are the days of judging

---

1 Clive Staples Lewis, *Reflections on the Psalms* (Orlando, FL: Harcourt Inc., 1958), 45.

the people in front of me at church, swaying back and forth, unintentionally obstructing my view of the screen and stage. I used to angrily mutter at them, "Get a prayer closet!" when they had the audacity to interfere with my preferred posture. Maybe you can relate.

Today, however, I wish to encourage, maybe even *challenge*, you to employ more bodily expression in public worship. I know this is a bit uncomfortable, and I'm aware that some Fives equate *expressive* worship with *excessive* worship, but this expression is about more than just feeling more bodily freedom. The brilliant BibleProject creators and self-identified Type Fives, Tim Mackie and Jon Collins, provide a rather intriguing insight on the ancient Jewish *Shema* prayer which is: "You shall love the LORD your God with all your heart and with all your soul and with all your might."[2]

Mackie and Collins explain that "soul" in this prayer is an unfortunate English translation. The Hebrew word that gets translated into "soul" is *nephesh*, or *throat*—a term used to describe our living, breathing, physical being—

> Clapping, bowing, lifting hands, shouting, and dancing are not only enjoyable but also serve as key elements of spiritual formation.

the place where our breath (which is also tied to *spirit*) meets our flesh and is released into the world. For example, when the Israelites were complaining about being hungry and thirsty in the desert they said, "Our [*nephesh*] has dried up."[3] One of the most famous verses of all time reads, "As the deer pants for the water, so my [*nephesh*] pants after you."[4] Mackie and Collins conclude, to "love the LORD your God … with all your soul"[5] is not actually a call to worship God with our spirit alone but also in concert with our physical body.[6]

The rest of the Psalms back this up: Psalm 47:1 calls for the act of clapping hands; 95:6 prompts us to bow down in worship; 134:2 encourages lifting up our hands

---

2   Deuteronomy 6:5

3   Numbers 11:6

4   Psalm 42:1

5   Deuteronomy 6:5

6   "Nephesh (Soul)." BibleProject, https://bibleproject.com/explore/video/nephesh-soul/ (accessed May 2, 2024).

in praise; 33:1 exhorts us to shout for joy; and 149:3 invites us to praise His name with dancing. These and many other verses collectively emphasize the vibrant and physical nature of worship, urging us to engage our entire being in adoration.

The Good News for Investigators is that although it may sound physically tiring, engaging your body in acts of worship will actually create a deeper connection with God. Much like physical activity enhances your brain and triggers endorphin release, physical expressions of worship such as clapping, bowing, lifting hands, shouting, and dancing are not only enjoyable but also serve as key elements of spiritual formation. Even on days when you might not feel inclined to physically express your faith, the deliberate action of raising your hands or kneeling—or even including other sensory aids like music, candles, or incense—can guide your heart and mind toward more holistic worship.

God absolutely loves when you worship Him with your mind. (And He notices, along with you, when the Sunday preacher seems to have forgotten to do that in their preparation!) He sees the way you observe insights in the Scriptures and ponder profound truths. But don't forget that there are other ways to experience Him. As Pastor Matthew Brown says in *A Book Called YOU*, "Not every song and not every sermon needs to be dissected. Sometimes you just need to feel what God has to say. Sometimes you just need to experience where the Spirit is moving."[7]

→ Pray

Father, help me to embrace the freedom to worship You with every part of my being. I recognize that physical expression can be a powerful form of spiritual formation. Therefore, remove any fear or hesitation within that holds me back from fully expressing my worship—whether I'm alone or in the company of others.

---

7   Matthew Stephen Brown, *A Book Called YOU: Understanding the Enneagram from a Grace-Filled, Biblical Perspective* (Nashville, TN: W Publishing, 2021), 101.

Day 24 Reflections:

Reflect on a moment when you felt a deep emotional connection during worship. How did your body instinctively respond (or want to respond), and if you allowed it to happen, how did this response enhance your experience of God?

Have you ever held back from expressing yourself physically in worship because it felt awkward, inauthentic, or unnecessary? What barriers do you face?

Pastor Matthew Brown encourages us not to dissect every song or sermon but to sometimes just feel what God is saying. How can embracing this advice be a good thing for you?

➔ Respond

The Psalms call for physical acts of worship such as clapping, bowing, shouting, lifting hands, and dancing. Which one of these actions can you incorporate into your private or corporate worship to deepen your connection with God?

Fives in Love

There is no fear in love, but perfect love casts out fear. For fear has to do with punishment, and whoever fears has not been perfected in love.

—1 John 4:18

INVESTIGATORS STAND ON THE EDGE OF THE vast, unknown wilderness of love, intrigued yet hesitant to step into its depths. Love's journey is especially daunting for Fives. Unlike other personality types, they approach love with a blend of fascination and fear, torn between the desire for connection and the comfort of solitude: *Do I really need love, or would I be happier on my own?* Fabulous in the abstract, love gets harder in reality.

Trust is a particularly high hurdle for them, and long-term commitment comes at a higher cost. Naturally cautious, Fives constantly wrestle with the fear of being overwhelmed by the intensity of love. They are skeptical in the early stages, always on guard for hidden agendas or expectations they

> Rather than love, than money, than fame, give me truth.
>
> —Henry David Thoreau[1]

---

1   Henry David Thoreau, *Walden* (Boston, MA: Houghton Mifflin, 1882), 510.

may not be able to fulfill, often stemming from a deep-seated belief in their inherent unworthiness.

When seeking a partner, Fives typically seek someone who respects their autonomy and doesn't pressure them to socialize more than they're comfortable with. However, they also value partners who can gently coax them out of their shells, encouraging them to savor life's moments, and once healthy Fives are in a relationship, they bring a multitude of benefits. For instance, One-to-One Fives, or those with a heavier Four wing, may resemble romantic Fours to some extent. Generally speaking, though, all healthy Fives are kind, loyal, and deeply committed. Since mental connection often precedes emotional and physical intimacy for them, they're drawn to partners with whom they share common interests or who are open to engaging in intellectual conversations and may talk for hours if the topic concerns a passion of theirs.[2] There's also no better confidante than a Five, and there's no need to worry about them overstepping boundaries or intruding on your privacy.

While Fives tend to limit their social lives, they really enjoy spending quality time with their partner. When healthy,

> Fabulous in the abstract, love gets harder in reality.

they will balance alone time with caring for loved ones, and because they are naturally observant, discerning a partner's needs comes naturally, leading to thoughtful gifts, literally and otherwise. Competent and resourceful, they will always bring wise counsel and sound advice and do a fantastic job of creating space for their partner's emotions without getting stuck in them, offering an objective perspective and off-beat humor to help their partner through life's biggest challenges.

Even though they may not say "I love you" as much as other types, their love is expressed in more nonverbal ways, such as quality time or acts of service. And while not as emotional in the moment, their feelings tend to bloom more naturally when alone. What's fascinating about Fives is how their affection for someone can blossom from a small seedling into a towering tree without the

---

2   Stephanie Barron Hall, *The Enneagram in Love: A Roadmap for Building and Strengthening Romantic Relationships* (Emeryville, CA: Rockridge Press, 2020), 57-58.

need for many words or prolonged personal contact.[3] When it comes to the physical aspect of the relationship, Fives are not particularly touchy-feely, but they still crave physical intimacy with their partner as a way of escaping their analytical minds and feeling bonded to the person they trust.

The Good News for Investigators is "there is no fear in love, but perfect love casts out fear."[4] The apostle John assures you that when you experience the depth of God's perfect love toward you, all fear—of "messing it up" or others' falsity—dissipates. His unconditional love is not based on fleeting emotions but on the objective truth that you have been redeemed and belong to Him. So surrender your fears and insecurities to God, allowing Him to fill you with His perfect love so that you can be free to love others—and the world. While loving others is always a risk, it's always a risk worth taking.

→ Pray

Father, I wrestle with the blend of fascination and fear when it comes to love. Fill me with the assurance that perfect love casts out fear and that Your unconditional love surrounds and sustains me. Help me surrender my fears and insecurities to You, trusting in Your love that sets me free to offer my full self to others without reservation.

---

3   Palmer, *The Enneagram in Love and Work*, 139.

4   1 John 4:18

Day 25 Reflections:

What unique qualities do you bring to a relationship, as described in the traits above?

Though love may have sounded good in the abstract, what aspect has been most challenging for you to navigate in reality?

Acknowledging the truth that "perfect love casts out fear," what lingering fear or insecurity about yourself or the relationship do you feel prompted to surrender today?

→ **Respond**

Take a bold step forward by practicing vulnerability with your partner—share something on your heart or mind to deepen intimacy and trust.

Blind Spots in Love

Love is patient and kind; love does not envy or boast; it is not arrogant

or rude. It does not insist on its own way; it is not irritable or resentful;

it does not rejoice at wrongdoing, but rejoices with the truth. Love bears

all things, believes all things, hopes all things, endures all things.

—1 Corinthians 13:4-7

YESTERDAY, WE EXPLORED HOW INVESTIGATORS APPROACH LOVE. Today, let's uncover some blind spots Fives may encounter in relationships. Much like checking your blind spot while driving, this may be challenging, but it can offer crucial insights for growth and relationship improvement. To categorize some of the blind spots that Fives may encounter, let's refer to 1 Corinthians 13:4-7 and explore the apostle Paul's timeless teaching on love in his first letter to the Corinthian church.

> The only thing worse than being blind is having sight but no vision.
>
> —Helen Keller[1]

---

1   Tyler Reagin, *Leading Things You Didn't Start: Winning Big When You Inherit People, Places, and Possibilities* (Colorado Springs: WaterBrook, 2021), 108.

Love is not arrogant. Fives may feel an urge at times to assert their expertise or prove they are right, potentially emitting an aura of intellectual arrogance. This may manifest in behaviors reminiscent of Eights, such as forcefully asserting their knowledge, interrupting others, or appearing condescending in an attempt to gain a sense of superiority.

Love is not rude. Torn between the desire for connection and the need to recharge, Fives may inadvertently come across as aloof or dismissive and struggle to remove the "Do Not Disturb" sign, leaving others feeling neglected. Interactions with a stressed Five may be brief, with a subtle message of dismissal: "You can go away now."[2] Communicating needs *in the moment* can clarify your intentions and prevent misunderstandings. Otherwise, constant emotional unavailability may drive a partner to seek fulfillment elsewhere.

It's important to recognize that silence can be perceived as rudeness, especially in emotionally charged situations. Conflict can drain a Five's energy, leading them to withdraw and gather their thoughts in isolation. While it may seem like avoidance helps prevent regrettable statements, healthy communication entails being available and vulnerable with your partner—and of course, vulnerability brings us back to letting emotions be felt and expressed to these trusted people and partners.

> Your capacity to love is not limited just because you are a Five.

Love does not insist on its own way. Fearing depletion of energy and resources, Fives may resist spending money on date nights or reject spontaneous requests from their partner. Rather than fostering mutual dependency, relying on each other for support and assistance during times of need, Fives may default to a mindset of "I'll take care of myself, and you take care of yourself." Additionally, because their "castle" is the primary place of security, they may become bossy at home, seeking control over household matters or dictating the relationship's agenda.[3]

Love is not irritable. Fives can become increasingly irritable under pressure. When feeling pressured, they may first hoard their time and resources, then become

---

2 Palmer, *The Enneagram in Love and Work*, 141-142.

3 Ibid., 137.

passive-aggressive, and finally resort to sarcastic, critical, or cynical remarks. And a Five who is overly-dependent on their partner to be the emotional lifeline may become possessive if they fear abandonment or betrayal.

As you reflect on these blind spots, remember they don't define you entirely—they're areas where growth is possible. Consider them not only as a diagnostic tool but also as a scorecard to track the progress you've made. As you remain mindful of these blind spots, here are proactive steps to enhance your relationship with your partner immediately: validate their emotions (and acknowledge your own), express your thoughts openly *before* overanalyzing them, and have communication check-ins regularly. Take the initiative to reach out to them first, engage in physical activities together to stay connected to your body, and be generous with your time, energy, and finances. Remember, your capacity to love is *not* limited just because you are a Five: if you invest generously, you'll yield significant returns.

The Good News for Investigators is that in the light of Jesus' life of sacrificial love, we can see our blind spots clearly. Through Jesus, the multi-faceted love of the triune Godhead described in 1 Corinthians 13 has been made visible to us. Just as a diverse spectrum of bright colors shine through a crystal prism, so too do the patience, kindness, truth, and enduring love of the Father shine through the Son with magnificent glory. If you have seen and tasted this radiant love, go and love others in the same way today.

→ Pray

Father, I humbly recognize my blind spots and seek Your help. Give me the strength to validate my partner's emotions, communicate openly, and act with generosity. Help me remember that Your love knows no bounds and that investing in my relationships will bring great rewards. In light of Your sacrificial love for me, may I mirror that love to others today.

Day 26 Reflections:

Which blind spot do you believe you've made noticeable progress in addressing within your relationships?

Which blind spot do you feel would benefit the most from additional growth and attention?

Looking at the proactive steps outlined, which specific action do you feel drawn to work on to strengthen your relationships?

> ### ➜ Respond
>
> Spoil your partner with material or experiential luxuries. Consider investing in a new mattress, planning a vacation together, or upgrading your vehicle or home.[4] If those options aren't financially feasible right now, my friend Kristen Yeh suggests more affordable alternatives, such as planning a creative date, picking up their favorite coffee on your way home, or indulging in something you wouldn't normally do.

---

4   Cron and Stabile, *The Road Back to You*, 186-187.

Wisdom Found Us

In the beginning was the [Logos], and the [Logos] was with God, and

the [Logos] was God. He was in the beginning with God. All things

were made through him, and without him was not any thing made

that was made. In him was life, and the life was the light of men.

—John 1:1-4

ACCORDING TO ANCIENT GREEK PHILOSOPHY, THE TERM *Logos* held significant importance. First introduced by the philosopher Heraclitus, *Logos* took on the meaning of a rational divine intelligence. Later, the Stoics adopted *Logos* as a foundational concept for their legal and moral frameworks, anticipating that alignment with this universal, divine force would yield freedom, happiness, and harmony.[2]

> I want to know all God's thoughts; all the rest are just details.
>
> –Albert Einstein[1]

Fast-forward hundreds of years to the era of apostle and Gospel-writer John, who

---

1   Dede Weldon Casad, *Traffic of the Mind: Determining and Acting Upon the Driving Forces of Our Lives* (Mustang, OK: Tate Publishing & Enterprises, LLC, 2010), 26.

2   "Glossary Definition: Logos." PBS. Accessed June 20, 2024. https://www.pbs.org/faithandreason/theogloss/logos-body.html.

chose to present Jesus as the *Logos*, which is ultimately translated as "the Word" in our English Bibles. To the surprise of the Greeks, this *Logos* of John's took on human form: "And the *[Logos]* became flesh and dwelt among us."[3] As French philosopher Luc Ferry said, ancient thinkers found it inconceivable that a mere mortal could embody the Logos.[4]

But Jesus didn't look or sound like your typical philosopher. While the Greeks operated on a hierarchical structure, with free-born men (who could become philosophers, craftsmen, and warriors) on top, and slaves at the bottom, Jesus introduced the radical notion of equality: "[Jesus], though he was in the form of God, did not count equality with God a thing to be grasped, but emptied himself, by taking the form of a servant, *being born in human likeness … .*"[5] The idea of a servant-philosopher getting His hands dirty, washing the feet of His students, would have seemed upside down. Sacrificing yourself for your social inferiors would have seemed even more ludicrous.

> Jesus is not a concept to comprehend, but a radical person to be encountered.

That is why the growth path for a Five must include a transformative shift in how you perceive and engage with truth. Jesus is not a *concept* to comprehend, but a radical *person* to be encountered. Author Jesse Eubanks points out that even though Christians believe in a Trinitarian, relational God, Fives may still reduce Him at times to a set of theological concepts. Systematic theology and Bible study can quickly replace relational engagement and cover over Jesus' radical, topsy-turvy way of life. In the same way that reading a book about skiing is not the same as actually experiencing the thrill and sensations of the slopes, studying *about* God is not the same thing as *knowing* God experientially.[6] In your moments of silence and solitude, how difficult have you found it to simply relax your mind and open up your body, heart, and spirit to a much deeper, experiential, and satisfying experience with a *personal* Savior?

---

3   John 1:14

4   Luc Ferry, *Learning to Live: A User's Manual* (Edinburgh: Canongate Books, 2010), 60.

5   Philippians 2:6-7

6   Eubanks, *How We Relate*, 169.

The Good News for Investigators is that Christianity offers the world something more than a profound *idea* or set of *ideals*; it invites us to know a compelling *person* to trust. As pastor Timothy Keller said, "When God decided to send salvation, he didn't send an airtight argument; he sent an airtight person. He didn't send an abstract principle; he sent a human being."[7]

This changes everything. For the Investigator, it means that true fulfillment cannot be sought in words on a page but can be found in the Logos who came searching for us. Consider the Three Wise Men—Zoroastrian astronomers who did not perceive the stars merely as the culmination of their intellectual fascination but as guiding lights that could lead one to uncover the secrets of the universe.[8] They traveled a very long journey to—surprise!—bow their knees before neither magic nor philosophy, but a young child.

Justin Martyr (100–165 AD), an early Church philosopher and apologist, serves as a great example of today's final important shift for Fives: more than becoming a thinker or teacher, Fives must become a *witness*. After trying out Stoicism and Platonism, his heart was kindled with a love of Christ when he heard of the incredible testimonies of the early saints. This ultimately compelled Justin to become a *martyr* (which means "witness") himself, and was eventually beheaded for acting out his beliefs courageously.

Like Justin, don't settle for being someone who merely thinks on and expounds your beliefs but become one who lives them out publicly as a witness, embodying the transformative power of the *Logos* to those watching from within and without the church. May your life speak volumes about the reality of a living faith that goes beyond intellectual understanding, inviting others into an exciting and dynamic relationship with the Word made flesh.

---

7   PodScripts Co. "Timothy Keller Sermons Podcast by Gospel in Life - Elijah and the Voice Transcript and Discussion." Podscripts. Accessed June 20, 2024. https://podscripts.co/podcasts/timothy-keller-sermons-podcast-by-gospel-in-life/elijah-and-the-voice.

8   Matthew 2:1-12

→ Pray

Father, thank You for sending Your Son, Jesus, who was wisdom personified. As one who often gets stuck in my head, open my heart up more to experience the depths of Your love. Help me to become a witness rather than just a teacher, so that others may be drawn to You through not only my words but also my actions.

Day 27 Reflections:

Contemplate Timothy Keller's assertion that Christianity offers not just profound ideas but an airtight person to trust in. How does this perspective influence your approach to faith?

Explore the significance of experiential knowledge versus intellectual understanding. How can you shift from mere theological comprehension to a deeper, relational engagement with God?

Think about the distinction between teaching about beliefs and living them out as a witness. In what ways can you direct others to Jesus through bold and courageous actions?

→ Respond

Begin a regular journaling practice, pouring out your thoughts to God in an intimate encounter. Share your heart, not just ideas, and let your journal become a sacred space for continuous conversation with your Creator.

Day 28:

Doubting Thomas

So the other disciples told him, "We have seen the Lord." But he said to them, "Unless I see in his hands the mark of the nails, and place my finger into the mark of the nails, and place my hand into his side, I will never believe."

—John 20:25

DO YOU REQUIRE A LITTLE MORE EVIDENCE, or direct personal experience, with something before you believe? As an Investigator, *doubt* is most likely an old companion of yours. Perhaps you have even thought of yourself as (or been called) a "doubting Thomas"? After Jesus rose from the dead and appeared to the disciples in the upper room, they told their friend Thomas, who had been absent at the time, that they had seen the risen Lord with their own eyes. Thomas, knowing that dead people tend to stay that way, remained skeptical. He said to them, "Unless I see in his hands the mark of the nails, and place

> I do not seek to understand in order that I may believe, but I believe in order that I may understand.
>
> —Anselem[1]

---

1   Philip Schaff and David Schley, *History of the Christian Church* (New York: C. Scribner's Sons, 1926), 602.

my finger into the mark of the nails, and place my hand into his side, I will never believe."[2]

Like Thomas, Fives aren't into wishful thinking. They have every itch to *believe* like the rest of us but need to back up what their hearts want through personal observation and physical proof. It wasn't sufficient for Thomas to take his friends at their word, and I imagine that some of his friends may have even harassed him a bit for not trusting them. Some might have even equated his *doubt* with *disbelief*.

There are still many Christians and communities today who have very little tolerance for doubt. It seems the number is growing of churches, campus ministries, seminaries, and even entire denominations who are determined to be curiosity killers. You have likely been told to simply "have more faith," by someone in a place like this. These environments can be incredibly challenging for Fives who need a safe space to wrestle with their doubts. They do this, not because they don't or don't want to believe, but precisely because they do.

> Your doubts don't have to lead to a dead end but can be stepping stones to fulfilling a greater purpose in your life.

Anselem, the eleventh-century Christian philosopher, coined the phrase "faith seeking understanding" as an alternative to someone having "blind faith."[3] Sir Francis Bacon, the seventeenth-century English philosopher, followed suit by saying, "It is true that a little philosophy inclineth man's mind to atheism, but depth in philosophy bringeth men's minds about to religion."[4] Because these thought leaders explored the tough questions of their day, their faith became much stronger and substantive—and their impact on other thoughtful people reverberates to this day.

The only caveat in this argument for healthy doubt is that, at some point, every skeptic needs to put their trust in some belief system. We cannot live in the realm

---

2 John 20:25

3 Thomas Williams, "Anselm of Canterbury." *Stanford Encyclopedia of Philosophy*, July 16, 2023. https://plato.stanford.edu/entries/anselm/#FaiSeeUndChaPurAnsThePro.

4 Susan Orr, *Jerusalem and Athens: Reason and Revelation in the Work of Leo Strauss* (United Kingdom: Rowman & Littlefield, 1995), 54.

of ideas and, whether we know it or not, are constantly making choices based on well-founded belief. David Hume, the Scottish philosopher and leader of skepticism, taught that we can't treat all worldviews with the same level of doubt because life compels us to make decisions every day, whether we want to or not. Hume's challenge, even from such a non-Christian perspective, urges all of us to acknowledge that pure skepticism is unsustainable; at some point, we all must lean on a belief system as the basis for our life and decisions.[5]

The great C.S. Lewis adds that skeptics who claim to be able to stand back and "see through" all truth claims are self-refuting. Lewis says the purpose of seeing through something, like a window, is to see what's beyond it. If you keep "seeing through," then everything eventually becomes transparent, and you find yourself in a dull, invisible world.[6]

The Good News for Investigators is just as Jesus didn't reject or chastise Thomas for his doubts, neither will He do so to you. Instead, He invites doubting Thomases to come closer and put their doubts to the test. When Jesus appears to Thomas, He says, "Put your finger here, and see my hands; and put out your hand, and place it in my side. Do not disbelieve, but believe."[7] After seeing and touching the scars with his own eyes, Thomas declares, "My Lord and my God!"[8] Legend has it that this "doubting" Thomas became one of the world's strongest believers, traveling to India and founding the Christian church there.[9] Wear your moniker of "doubting" as a point of pride: like Thomas, your doubts don't have to lead to a dead end but can be stepping stones to fulfilling a greater purpose in your life.

---

5   Bryan Magee, *The Story of Philosophy* (New York: Dorling Kindersley Limited, 2016).

6   C.S. Lewis and Michael Ward, *The Abolition of Man: C.S. Lewis's Classic Essay on Objective Morality: A Critical Edition by Michael Ward* (United States: TellerBooks, 2017), 102.

7   John 20:27

8   John 20:28

9   George Nedungatt, "The Apocryphal 'Acts of Thomas' and Christian Origins in India." *Gregorianum* 92, no. 3 (2011): 533-557. Available at: https://www.jstor.org/stable/43922416 (accessed May 4, 2024).

> **➜ Pray**
>
> Father, help me to continue chasing a "faith seeking understanding," rather than shying away from hard questions. Give me the wisdom to discern between rigorous, healthy skepticism and blind faith. Just as You welcomed Thomas' doubts and led him to a deeper understanding, may my doubts lead me closer to You and Your purpose for my life.

Day 28 Reflections:

What's your relationship with doubt? Which aspects of your faith have been most challenging to reconcile with doubt?

Have you experienced criticism or dismissal when expressing doubts in your family or faith community? How did it affect you?

How can you create a safe space for exploring doubts within your faith community, fostering open dialogue among believers?

> **➜ Respond**
>
> Initiate a discussion or organize a small group within your faith community dedicated to exploring doubts and questions openly.

Turn Daydreams into Reality

[Aaron] shall speak for you to the people, and he shall be your

mouth, and you shall be as God to him. And take in your

hand this staff, with which you shall do the signs.

—Exodus 4:16-17

1N 1901, A YOUNG BOY NAMED WALTER was born on the northwest side of Chicago. Walter grew up spending most days "in his own head," often putting his dreams into pictures. He took his first job as a commercial illustrator at the age of eighteen and went on to become the most famous animator, voice actor, and film producer ever. Walt Disney pioneered the American animation industry and won a record twenty-two Oscars. His imagination was the springboard for some of our culture's most beloved stories, the greatest amusement park franchise in the world, and one of the most dominant businesses in history.[2]

> [Fives] may awaken one day to realize that they have not lived a life—they have been preparing for one.
>
> —Russ Hudson[1]

---

1   Riso and Hudson, *The Wisdom of the Enneagram*, 218-219.

2   Biography.com Editors. "Walt Disney Biography." Biography.com, January 7, 2022. https://www.biography.com/business-leaders/walt-disney.

Many Investigators possess a Disney-like imagination: crafting beautiful music, creating stunning works of visual art, or writing compelling novels; they are the researchers and scientists who find new paths around old roadblocks and epiphanies where before were only dead ends. However, if these creations remain confined within the Five's mind, they'll never be played by an instrument, grace a canvas, or reach publication. Imagine if Disney's iconic films had never been shared with the world, or if his visionary amusement parks had never materialized. What if he had merely awaited inspiration, finding endless reasons to delay transforming his daydreams into reality?

A common roadblock to realizing your dreams is not granting yourself permission to dream big in the first place. Early in life, Fives may have experienced the pain of rejection by

> Your legacy will not be determined by what you dream but by what you do.

not having their needs met or aspirations supported, and as a reaction to this early wounding, they can unconsciously block up feelings inside, and keep them from rising to the surface. Rather than going after what they want, they may talk themselves out of doing something they are passionate about, downsizing their dreams, thinking they don't deserve to make any wishes.[3]

In contrast, when Type Sevens embrace the *pleasure* of a big idea, they ignite it with enthusiasm, using that excitement to propel them into action. If Fives embark on this growth path toward Seven, they'll allow the delight they find in a specific dream to propel them forward with a sense of urgency to see it realized and shared with the world.[4] As enthusiasm builds, they can overcome the next obstacle: getting sidetracked by trivial pursuits. While Fives often enjoy things like books, board games, video games, puzzles, and podcasts, they must guard against these good things becoming a distraction and substitute for greater pursuits.

The final hurdle for Fives in pursuing their dreams is resignation—accepting defeat before even starting, daunted by the perceived enormity of the energy and

---

3   Sandra Maitri, *The Spiritual Dimension of the Enneagram: Nine Faces of the Soul* (United States: Penguin Publishing Group, 2000), 208-209.

4   Naranjo, *Character and Neurosis*, 99.

resources required for success. Average Fives often feel a lack of agency, sensing themselves as limited and powerless to achieve their aspirations. Isolated with their thoughts and doubting they'll receive the help and support they need, their hearts are strewn with dormant dreams.

The Good News for Investigators is that dreamers aren't expected to influence the world on their own. Although Walt Disney was perceived to be a Type A leader, those who knew him said he was shy, self-deprecating, and insecure about his abilities. He was able to accomplish so much largely because of an older, business-savvy brother, Roy, who helped turn Walt's dream into reality.[5]

Consider Moses in the book of Exodus. Initially, the great liberator of Israel felt inadequate to lead, rejecting God's job offer. But God graciously provided Moses with his brother, Aaron, to do some of the heavy lifting. Not only that, but God gave Moses a staff, with which he performed miracles and represented divine authority and power. Pay attention! God wants to give you a staff and a partner: Look around to see whom God has already put in your life. Your potential for influencing the world will likely not be limited by others, nor your boundless creativity, but by whether or not you have the courage to ask someone to help turn those dreams into reality. Ultimately, your legacy will not be determined by what you *dream* but by what you *do*.

→ Pray

Father, give me the power to overcome the roadblocks of doubt and resignation that hinder me from pursuing the dreams You've put in my heart. Though I tend to do things alone, help me to recognize and embrace the support of others, as Moses did with Aaron. Thank You for the people You've placed in my life to assist me on this journey.

---

5 "Walt Disney." Biography.com, August 21, 2020, https://www.biography.com/business-fig-ure/walt-disney.

Day 29 Reflections:

What do you enjoy about being a dreamer? How has God already used your imagination to add color and depth to the world?

Consider a dream you've begun pursuing that remains unfinished or has the potential to grow. What steps can you take to further develop it?

What is the biggest obstacle that tends to get in the way of you chasing your dreams? Who can you ask to support you in overcoming this challenge?

→ Respond

Reach out to at least one person in your support network who can offer guidance, encouragement, or assistance in accomplishing an unfinished dream.

Day 30:

Just Ship It

And he who had received the five talents came forward, bringing five talents more, saying, "Master, you delivered to me five talents; here, I have made five talents more." His master said to him, "Well done, good and faithful servant. You have been faithful over a little; I will set you over much. Enter into the joy of your master."

—Matthew 25:20-21

"JUST SHIP IT" IS A COMMON BUSINESS phrase often used by activator personalities that many Investigators tend to dislike: this push for completing tasks or projects quickly, even if they're not fully polished, is a classic pet peeve of this type. Fives are much less concerned with monthly quotas or impressing higher-ups, preferring to take their time, ensuring they understand how each project fits into the bigger picture. As a result, when Fives *aren't* on the team or sufficiently heard, there can be major issues like broken websites, error-filled emails, miscommunication, and defective products.

> **Done is better than perfect.**
>
> –Greg McKeown[1]

---

1   Greg McKeown, *Essentialism: The Disciplined Pursuit of Less* (New York: Crown Business, 2014), 199.

That being said, it's crucial to recognize where Fives fall on the spectrum of *thinking* versus *doing* and acknowledge the need for help in this area. While Eights follow the classic Silicon Valley *move fast and break things* approach and often pursue goals with a "fire, ready, aim" strategy, Fives typically find themselves taking the *move slow and do nothing* approach, endlessly trapped in an "aim, aim, aim" cycle. Alongside Type Fours and Nines, Fives tend to repress their doing. This trio prioritizes introspection, contemplation, and processing over action and would do well to remember that "done is better than perfect" and "perfect is the enemy of the good."

There are countless shows and movies featuring protagonists with private investigation boards in their homes, filled with pictures and clues. As the story progresses, they use a red string to connect unrelated bits of information and eventually find the connecting center and solve the mystery. Fives remind me of these investigators, enjoying hours staring at the board, refusing to eat, sleep, or leave until all the pins point the same direction.

In real life, however, Fives risk losing their jobs or relationships if they obsess over life or work's little puzzles and never attend team meetings. They may clash with their spouses if they keep neglecting household chores or relational bids for connection. That's why it's crucial not to let your superpower of planning lead to paralysis, whether at work or home. Whether researching a home appliance purchase or contemplating a career move, Fives can get stuck in preparation mode.

> Competency is wisdom in action.

It's been said that average Fives love both *pre*-flection and *re*flection, but just as there's no commonly used word for what comes between those two stages, there's a gap in the mind of a Five.[2] While you might not see yourself as a classic procrastinator, procrastination in the life of an Investigator often sounds like, "I still have a few more questions," or "I need to do a little more research." As a result, the painter never exhibits their work or the author never actually writes the book, the programmer never publishes the app, or the student never becomes a teacher.

---

2   Rohr and Ebert, *The Enneagram*, 127.

Consider Jesus' parable of the talents, where two servants are praised: those who, lacking some information and perhaps even fearfully, nevertheless put their master's money to work, investing their talents and seeing a return; the third servant, meanwhile is rebuked for their fear and laziness, choosing instead to bury the money.[3] Similarly, in our lives, when we allow fear or perfectionism to paralyze us, we miss out on opportunities to grow and contribute. We need to remember that God has entrusted us with talents and resources, and He expects us to use them in a timely fashion.

The Good News for Investigators is that God prioritizes *progress* over *perfection*. We are the "rough drafts" of our future selves, and despite being a work in progress, we are deeply loved by God. Our incompleteness doesn't diminish God's competence in placing us in this world. Let God redefine your understanding of competency. Competency is *wisdom in action*. Remember, there will always be someone who knows more or less than you, but God seeks out leaders who are willing to take action before they feel "ready." Today's action step is to "just ship it!" Far from advocating for laziness or haste, I am encouraging you to start sharing more of your "rough drafts" with others. By getting it off your "desk," you can test out the idea, receive feedback, observe its impact on others, and then fine-tune it. Don't view the finish line as acquiring more knowledge, but as the point where you can seize opportunities and take action.[4]

→ Pray

Father, help me navigate the balance between thinking and action. Give me the courage to move forward, embracing progress over perfection. Surround me with wise advisers who can help me apply my wisdom in practical ways. Redefine my understanding of competency, reminding me that becoming an expert means putting wisdom into action.

---

3   Matthew 25:14-30

4   Sarajane Case, *The Honest Enneagram: Know Your Type, Own Your Challenges, Embrace Your Growth* (Kansas City, MO: Andrews McMeel Publishing, 2020), 135.

Day 30 Reflections:

Describe a time when you resisted procrastination (remember: this can mean more "research" in your case) and simply took action. How did it feel, and what were the outcomes?

What procrastination habits do you find yourself falling into most frequently? How can you shift your mindset to prioritize action?

Reflect on a project or goal that you've been putting off. What small action can you take today to ship it and move it forward?

> **➜ Respond**
>
> Share an idea that is still in the works with someone you trust. Remember, you don't need to have all the answers or problems solved to feel competent or express it confidently.

The Beginning of Knowledge

The fear of the LORD is the beginning of knowledge;

fools despise wisdom and instruction.

—Proverbs 1:7

DID THE PHRASE "THE FEAR OF THE LORD" ever perplex you? I was relieved to find out that "fear" did not imply sheer terror, but rather deep respect and awe, like when you're climbing up a steep cliff and feel that mix of excitement and anxiety. The sort of fear that leads us to have less confidence in ourselves and more willingness to lean on the council of experts. Meanwhile, as Proverbs often reminds us, the fool is the one who rolls their eyes at someone offering wisdom and advice gained through experience.

> I know that I know nothing.
>
> —Socrates[1]

What's the antidote to all this foolishness? *Humility.* The realization and acceptance that not only are there gaps in your knowledge and experience, but *no amount* of knowledge can make you right one hundred percent of the time. As Pastor Matthew Brown says, "People are not better people when

---

1   Chestnut and Paes, *The Enneagram Guide to Waking Up*, 137.

they're smarter. They're just better at convincing themselves that what they're doing isn't wrong."[2]

As I mentioned on Day One, the Five's life verse should be: "Trust in the LORD with all your heart, and do not lean on your own understanding. In all your ways acknowledge him, and he will make straight your paths."[3] But actually following that advice is way easier said than done, because God's way feels way too simple, foolish, or even downright embarrassing at times. That is why Christ, the "wisdom of God,"[4] became a stumbling block to the Greek philosophers and the Hebrew fundamentalists. How could a humble, blue-collar, foot-washing Jew—who appeared too weak to save Himself on the cross—be the source of true knowledge and the path to humanity's salvation?

It seems that, to some extent, God set it up this way because He has a sense of humor. After all, Jesus delighted in the fact that the Father hides His ways from those who are wise in their own eyes and instead revealed them to little children.[5] God apparently intended to flip the script and ensure that no Greek (or Five!) "might boast in the presence of God."[6] As the apostle Paul explained to the church in Corinth, "God chose what is foolish in the world to shame the wise."[7] He goes on to remind us that "If anyone among you thinks that he is wise in this age, let him become a fool that he may become wise."[8]

> The path of humility lies in approaching the throne, not with sophistication but with childlike wonder.

In case you are wondering, yes, Paul suggests that even a Five, whose core fear is appearing *incompetent*, must become a fool in the eyes of the world. In this context, becoming a fool practically means letting go of the need to understand

---

2   Brown, *A Book Called YOU*, 100.

3   Proverbs 3:5-6

4   1 Corinthians 1:24

5   Matthew 11:25

6   1 Corinthians 1:29

7   1 Corinthians 1:27

8   1 Corinthians 3:18

and control everything, or trying to look and feel like you have it all figured out. It's saying, "I don't know" often. Just as the Ethiopian Eunuch told Stepehen, "How can I [know], unless someone guides me?"[9] The path of humility lies in approaching the throne, not with sophistication, but with childlike wonder, singing, "Be Thou my wisdom."[10] It's not banking on what you know, but marveling at what you don't: "Oh, the depth of the riches and wisdom and knowledge of God!"[11]

The Good News for Investigators is the invitation to deeper wisdom has been freely offered: "If you receive my words and treasure up my commandments with you, making your ear attentive to wisdom … then you will understand the fear of the LORD and find the knowledge of God."[12] The challenge and invitation is there for you to seek out others' wisdom and experience to guide you, rather than relying solely on your own understanding to make decisions and handle challenges. Let go of everything you think you know and allow God to take you into deeper mysteries full of reverence and awe.

➔ Pray

Father, I come before You in full humility, recognizing the depth of Your wisdom. Thank You for the invitation to come to a deeper place of understanding, one that seems upside down in the eyes of the world. Forgive any pride or arrogance within me and keep me from relying solely on my own understanding and help me to trust You completely.

---

9   Acts 8:31

10   "Be Thou My Vision." *Hymnal.net*, https://www.hymnal.net/en/hymn/ns/345 (accessed April 24, 2024).

11   Romans 11:33

12   Proverbs 2:1-5

Day 31 Reflections:

Have you ever dismissed wisdom or advice from others, only to realize later that it could have been valuable? What did you learn from that experience?

How has your perception of wisdom changed as you've grown older and gained more knowledge?

What do you think Paul meant by becoming a fool in the eyes of the world? What does this look like practically?

→ Respond

Step out of your comfort zone and put yourself in a setting that might make you look foolish. Exercise humility by receiving guidance from others, even if they seem less experienced.

Modern Monks

And the Word became flesh and dwelt among us, and we have seen his

glory, glory as of the only Son from the Father, full of grace and truth.

—John 1:14

MONKS HAVE NOT ALWAYS BEEN VIEWED FAVORABLY in some Christian circles because of their secluded way of life. But if you take a closer look at their contributions over the millennia, you can see how they have helped keep both spiritual and cultural traditions alive, particularly during periods of persecution or cultural disintegration. It was the monastic communities who—through dedicating themselves to prayer, contemplation, writing, and teaching—preserved Church teachings and history.

> If you have knowledge, let others light their candles in it.
>
> —Margaret Fuller[1]

Investigators are the modern-day monks of our culture. You play a crucial role in preserving and enriching the faith that has been passed down to us. For Fives, delving into the study of the Bible, immersing yourself in the original language of the text, conducting word or topic studies,

---

1 Cron, *The Story of You,* 143.

and consulting various resources or commentaries, serves as one of the most accessible and fulfilling spiritual disciplines.[2]

However, given that practices such as Bible study, prayer, journaling, and solitude deeply enrich the lives of Fives, there's a risk of becoming overly attached to these pursuits. Fives may find themselves off-balance if they begin to equate contemplative disciplines *to* the Christian life. Father Richard Rohr, founder of the aptly named Center for Action and Contemplation (note the need for both!), has expressed concern over numerous unhealthy Fives within the priesthood:

> Fives may find themselves off-balance if they begin to equate contemplative disciplines to the Christian life.

"Some of them are older than I am and are still not finished with their training for any service. You wonder: when will these people begin to do something for others and translate their knowledge into practice? First they have to go to Chicago and finish their degree in philosophy. Then they have to go to Rome to write a paper on the liturgy. Next they spend a year in Jerusalem and take up biblical and archaeological studies. They need the certainty of really having gotten the whole picture before they feel ripe for any undertaking. But that never happens, and so their flesh never touches the flesh of the world."[3]

What a poignant and evocative way to describe the problem: *their flesh never touches the flesh of the world.* In contrast, Rohr brings up another Catholic, Agnes, whom we all know as Mother Teresa. At eighteen years old, she joined a teaching order of nuns called the English Ladies, and from there, she was sent to teach geography at a high school in Calcutta, India. But young Agnes found herself drawn more to the slums behind the school and, after becoming director, began taking her students into the slum to care for the sick. But these short visits were not enough, so in 1946, she issued a public statement that she would be leaving the convent to go live among the poor.[4]

---

2   Sherrill, *The Enneagram for Spiritual Formation*, 74.

3   Rohr and Ebert, *The Enneagram*, 118.

4   Ibid., 131-132.

Even if most Fives never sense a call to live among the outcasts of society like Mother Teresa, her example is still humbling, inspiring and challenging all of us—and perhaps especially Fives—to consider leaving their "monastery," whether it be for a few hours or years, to make our physical presence available to people in need. Pastor AJ Sherrill says engaging in the spiritual discipline of serving can get you out of your head and into your hands: service opportunities may include volunteering with Habitat for Humanity, a soup kitchen, or an after-school program.[5] An often overlooked aspect of monastic life, both ancient and modern, is the commitment to hospitality toward the poor and needy. When healthy, these women and men are shining examples of disciples who aren't afraid to get their hands a little dirty.

The Good News for Investigators is that Jesus' flesh touched the world and lived among us.[6] He left the comfort of heaven and entered our human experience, exemplifying selfless love and service, healing the sick, and touching the untouchables. Ultimately, Jesus' greatest act of service was offering up His body on the cross, being fully depleted so that our life would be fully replenished. The incarnation is one of those cornerstone theological topics that Fives should not only feast on intellectually but also spend their whole lifetime working out. As you engage in acts of service, becoming the hands and feet of Jesus for those in need, you won't find yourself distant from God but enveloped in a profound realization of His nearness to you.

→ Pray

Father, thank You for sending Jesus to touch the world with His healing presence. Help me find balance in study and action. Keep me from becoming too attached to the spiritual disciplines I find satisfying and comforting, and inspire me to step out in service, following the example of those who have sacrificed so much to get me to where I am today.

---

5 Sherrill, *The Enneagram for Spiritual Formation*, 74.

6 John 1:14

Day 32 Reflections:

How has God used your enjoyment of the contemplative spiritual disciplines for the good of others?

Reflecting on Father Richard Rohr's warning about the potential pitfalls of knowledge without action, where do you recognize this tendency in your journey?

As you consider the example of Jesus' incarnation, His willingness to touch and serve humanity, where do you feel you can extend your supportive presence or offer physical assistance?

→ **Respond**

Find a person, group, or cause to regularly volunteer for or simply show up to offer moral support.

Wrestling with God

Then the man said, "Your name will no longer be Jacob, but Israel, because

you have struggled with God and with humans and have overcome."

—Genesis 32:28 NIV

INVESTIGATORS ARE MORE COMFORTABLE WRESTLING WITH *IDEAS* than people. When faced with a conflict or crisis of faith or relationship, average Fives often detach emotionally and intellectualize their experiences as a way to maintain a sense of control. Seeking an unbiased observer position can be helpful, but this intellectualization can ultimately lead to harmful determinism. This may result in a sense of resignation, viewing all events as inevitable and therefore not worth your energy trying to change.

> Wrestling with God is a sign of intimacy. You can't wrestle with someone you're far away from.
>
> –Jon Acuff

Fives try to solve conflict by thinking things through rather than expressing emotion. In contrast, other types, such as Sixes, like my wife, approach conflict with emotional intensity and honesty, ready to lay everything out on the table. I wish I had known this before we got married because my strategy caused major problems after experiencing the long road of infertility. For years, Lindsey cried and cried, unable to believe we'd ever see a miracle, and to this day, still no miracle. I, on the other hand, showed no emotion. I told her not to worry, that God had a plan—but this was just an unconscious strategy to temporarily sweep things under the rug. In so doing, I suppressed Lindsey's pain, failed to offer God's presence, and held fast to stoicism when I should have been sowing tears.

Thankfully, we joined a small group of believers who felt stuck in various ways. During one of our sessions, the leader pointed his finger at me and sternly said, "David was a man who grieved and was called a man after God's own heart. You haven't done that." It sounds harsh, but those were the words I needed to wake up. It had never occurred to me that being a man after God's own heart meant wrestling with Him over my infertility struggle. For the next year, I immersed myself in the Psalms, continually shocked that David was praised rather than reprimanded for bringing his pains, complaints, heartaches—and if I'm being honest, *drama*—to God.

> Confrontation, whether with God or our loved ones, is a sign of commitment, not indifference.

As we discussed on Day 22, C.S. Lewis was forced to have his own wrestling match with God after losing his dearest wife to cancer. Madeleine L'Engle, author of *A Wrinkle in Time*, shares her reaction in the Foreword to *A Grief Observed*:

"I am grateful, too, to Lewis for having the courage to yell, to doubt, to kick at God with angry violence. This is part of a healthy grief not often encouraged. It is helpful indeed that C.S. Lewis, who has been such a successful apologist for Christianity, should have the courage to admit doubt about what he has so superbly proclaimed. It gives us permission to admit our own doubts, our own angers and anguishes, and to know that they are part of the soul's growth."[1]

This sentiment echoes the essence of a famous wrestling match in Scripture. In the darkness near the Jabbok River, Jacob was attacked and struggled until dawn. In a stalemate, the opponent dislocated Jacob's hip, yet Jacob persisted,

---

1   C.S. Lewis, *A Grief Observed* (United Kingdom: HarperCollins, 2001), XVI.

demanding, "I will not let you go until you bless me."[2] To which God said, "Your name shall no longer be called Jacob, but Israel, for you have striven with God and with men, and have prevailed."[3] In this deeply formative story of a nation's founding, we see a core belief formed: that God delights in people who aren't afraid to strive and struggle—after all, *Israel* means "one who struggles with God." As the rabbis would later say, *the dust from their struggle rose up to the Throne of Glory.*[4]

The Good News for Investigators is that, like a burnt offering rising to God, your honest struggle is welcomed by God, even (or especially) if it means yelling, doubting, or expressing frustration. Your doubts, anger, grief, and disappointment are not too much for Him. Confrontation, whether with God or our loved ones, is a sign of commitment, not indifference. Practice replacing your well-worded requests with raw emotion—God won't punish or abandon you, rather, you have a Father who is more than willing to step into the ring with you. As Jon Acuff says, "Wrestling with God is a sign of intimacy. You can't wrestle with someone you're far away from."[5]

→ Pray

Father, I find comfort in knowing You understand and embrace our struggles. I confess that I sometimes hesitate to bring my pains, complaints, and heartaches to You. Thank You for giving me permission to be brutally honest. I know You can handle it. As I wrestle with You, may I grow ever closer to You.

---

2   Genesis 32:25-30

3   Genesis 32:28

4   Lawrence Kushner, *God Was in This Place and I, I Did Not Know—25th Anniversary Ed: Finding Self, Spirituality and Ultimate Meaning* (Woodstock, VT: Jewish Lights Publishing, 2016), 71.

5   Jon Acuff. *"Wrestling with God is a sign of intimacy. You can't wrestle with someone you're far away from."* https://i.pinimg.com/736x/cb/b6/2c/cbb62c35b45738be1c8235302b1072d9–perfect-guy-wrestling.jpg. Accessed 23 June 2024.

Day 33 Reflections:

How does the quote "Wrestling with God is a sign of intimacy" challenge or affirm your view of your relationship with God?

Reflect on those close to you and how they handle struggles. Have you ever unintentionally dismissed their emotions or pain with intellectual explanations or platitudes?

Have you reflected on whether your response to conflict may come across as more indifferent than committed? How can you cultivate a mindset of confrontational intimacy to deepen your relationships?

→ Respond

Read Psalm 77 and observe how vulnerable and honest Asaph is with the Lord. After meditating on the Psalm, try offering a prayer to the Lord with the same level of honesty.

Get Out of Your Head

This "knowledge" puffs up, but love builds up.

—1 Corinthians 8:1

FILMMAKER AND TYPE FIVE PHIL VISCHER OFTEN says that Investigators are like computer hard drives.[2] Constantly reading and writing data, they encrypt their private information and emotions, then save everything into well-organized folders and subfolders. But there's only one problem with a hard drive according to Vischer—*it isn't a whole human being.*

> Fives can pontificate on what you know and perseverate over what you don't know.
>
> –Calhoun and Loughrige[1]

When Fives become more "machine" than human, knowledge becomes an idol—their source of power and security—and may even become a substitute for the comfort and support that others usually look for in relationships. All Fives are drawn to places where knowledge is stored and dispensed and to intellectually stimulating environments

---

1   Calhoun and Loughrige, *Spiritual Rhythms*, 142.

2   Jesse Eubanks and Lindsey Lewis, "#91: Your Desire to Be Competent with Phil Vischer (Type 5)." Enneagram Journey to Self-Discovery. Podcast audio, May 16, 2023.

and people. If someone doesn't make them feel intellectually challenged, it's really hard to stay engaged, and they may craft an echo chamber of their own thoughts to keep themselves interested and stimulated. Like an unhealthy Type Seven, who can become an adrenaline junky and only find meaning in the next exciting experience, average Fives can replace *living* with the electric surge that *learning* brings.[3]

Wanting to feel safe and in control, Fives use *compartmentalization* as a defense mechanism. They may save memories from the past, but delete any file extensions with strong feelings, making the process of recall less painful. They categorize their career, family, friendships, church community, and other commitments into separate folders on their mental drive, reducing stress and giving them the power to choose which files to access and when. However, in an unhealthy state, this rigid control can lead them to view relationships as mere files and folders—abstract concepts rather than living, breathing connections.

> Fives can replace living with the electric surge that learning brings.

As Vischer jokes, when a Five becomes detached from their flesh and blood bodies and hearts, and transforms into a "brain in a box," they become as cold as a computer chip. Their humor might sometimes take on a snarky tone and they will often exhibit a know-it-all attitude, using their knowledge to make others feel foolish. The more insecure they are, the more they will find it difficult to relate to other people, except through the role of The Expert or The Guru. Thus, they must carve out their own niche and double down on research to learn what no one else knows.[4] They can (typically unintentionally) embarrass or belittle others with statements like, "I'm surprised you didn't know that," or can undermine someone's excitement by saying things like, "So you're going to the beach? I was just reading the latest report on the ozone layer. Studies show that the chances of getting skin cancer have gone up by nearly one hundred percent."[5]

In light of these propensities, we should remember that the apostle Paul, one of Scripture's most brilliant writers, said: "This 'knowledge' puffs up, but love builds

---

3   Case, *The Honest Enneagram*, 142.

4   Riso and Hudson, *The Wisdom of the Enneagram*, 217.

5   Riso and Hudson, *Personality Types*, 195-196.

up."[6] He emphasizes that an over-pursuit of knowledge, whether about the nature of idols as in this passage or in general, can lead to pride and arrogance. Living a life primarily in your head may feel safe and comfortable, but it can hinder your ability to connect with and love others. The growth path for Fives is similar to that of the Tin Man in the Wizard of Oz—a journey to rediscover your heart and embrace the fullness of your humanity.

The Good News for Investigators is you are more than your ideas. To get out of your head this week, set aside moments each day to ask yourself, "What do I *feel*?" rather than "What do I *think*?" When engaging with others, remember that knowledge isn't the only currency. Strive to connect on deeper levels, beyond intellect, by engaging with their stories and experiences. Additionally, establish boundaries around your pursuit of knowledge to prevent it from dominating your life by dedicating more time to hobbies, social events, and group activities to enrich your human experience. The next time you feel like you are "losing your mind," remember that you are fully *human*. You are not a thinking head on a stick, but a beloved son or daughter who has been given a sensitive heart with deep desires, cravings, and longings for human connection.

→ Pray

Father, remind me that I am fully human, with desires, cravings, and emotions. Guide me back to You when I get lost in my head, detached from my heart. Show me that true security comes from You, not from what I know. Keep me humble, Lord, and lead me on the path of rediscovering the beauty of my humanity.

---

6   1 Corinthians 8:1

Day 34 Reflections:

Do you relate to the metaphor of being a thinking head on a stick? In what ways?

Have you ever caught yourself adopting a know-it-all attitude or unintentionally belittling others with your knowledge? How did it make you feel afterward?

What strategies do you find effective for getting out of your head and becoming a whole human being? How can you incorporate more of these into your daily life?

→ **Respond**

Take up a creative hobby such as painting, writing, or playing a musical instrument to tap into your emotions and creativity.

Orthopraxy vs. Orthodoxy

But be doers of the word, and not hearers only, deceiving yourselves.

—James 1:22

MIKE COSPER, A WRITER AND PODCASTER FOR *Christianity Today*, acknowledges that as an Investigator, focusing on orthodoxy is much easier than orthopraxy, which requires him to apply what he knows to his everyday life. The term "orthodoxy" pertains to correct doctrine, whereas "orthopraxy" involves putting those beliefs into correct action, and both are crucial in the life of faith.[2] When orthopraxy lacks orthodoxy, it results in activism without a solid theological foundation. Conversely, when orthodoxy lacks orthopraxy, faith becomes intellectualized with no real-world application. Balancing both ensures that faith is not just theoretical but lived out authentically.

> Love only has logic, only has meaning, when it takes the form of the cross.
>
> –Ann Voskamp[1]

Practical application can be difficult for Fives, who spend a great deal of time going on pleasurable mental

---

1   Ann Voskamp, *The Broken Way (with Bonus Content): A Daring Path Into the Abundant Life* (Grand Rapids, MI: Zondervan, 2016), 109.

2   "Orthodoxy: Search Online Etymology Dictionary." Etymology. Accessed June 22, 2024. https://www.etymonline.com/search?q=orthodoxy.

rabbit-trails throughout the day, but this superpower of knowledge acquisition can eventually become counterproductive. For example, a Five may lose a lot of sleep discovering a ground-breaking solution in their career field but be unable to solve their relationship problems.[3] They might be experts on the intricacies of ancient Egyptian history, the art of French cuisine, or the physics behind black holes but struggle with gaining (and keeping) employment.

Because Fives "tend to dwell in abstractions while at the same time avoiding concreteness,"[4] their loved ones may be looking for more tangible results from them. They need a partner who doesn't get caught up in impractical pursuits but offers to help with shared ground-level responsibilities such as childcare, running errands, transportation for the kids, and household maintenance.

A quote from author Bob Goff, shared earlier in the book but worth repeating, is, "I used to think being loved was the greatest thing to think about, but now I know love is never satisfied just thinking about it."[5] In other words, love is not theoretical, but deeply practical. The apostle James emphasized this long ago when he challenged the early Chrsitians to "be doers of the word, and not hearers only, deceiving yourselves."[6] The Bible itself was not written as an intellectual exercise; rather, it is a catalog of humanity's experiences with the Divine and their exhortations to radical transformation as a result of these encounters. The more mature our love for God, the quicker we will *do* what we've seen and heard. It's all too easy for Fives to absorb volumes of books or gigs of podcasts without stopping to consider what to do with that information *today*.

> When orthodoxy lacks orthopraxy, faith becomes intellectualized with no real-world application.

I've always found great pleasure in reading and discussing theology. Growing up, I was part of a church tradition that placed a high value on our understanding of orthodoxy, focusing more on theological debates than community engagement. However, my perspective shifted when I met Pastor Jamison, whose multiethnic

---

3   Riso and Hudson, *The Wisdom of the Enneagram*, 208-209.

4   Naranjo, *Character and Neurosis*, 100.

5   Goff, *Love Does*, 17.

6   James 1:22

church merged with the congregation I was shepherding in 2019. During our discussions at a local coffee shop about the potential merger, I found myself eager to discuss a theological position paper I had written, hoping to gauge our alignment on certain issues, but to my surprise, Pastor Jamison admitted that he hadn't delved deeply into the topic and couldn't answer all my questions.

At first, encounters like this can lead the intellectually-minded to look down on someone like Pastor Jamison. Yet upon further reflection, I realized that, despite the fact he had less expertise in that particular area of orthodoxy, his church was renowned in the city for its community involvement: they regularly visited those in jail, assisted the homeless, and were deeply engaged in their neighborhood. Meeting Pastor Jamison taught me a valuable lesson: orthodoxy alone is insufficient without orthopraxy. I was humbled by the realization that my correct beliefs don't matter unless they lead to practical action.

The Good News for Investigators is that God invites you and me into His unfolding plan of redemption as active participants, not mere observers. As image-bearers, we're called not only to understand His love but to reflect it in our actions. Jesus, our perfect example, demonstrated love through practical service, culminating in His sacrifice on the cross. As Ann Voskamp beautifully articulates, "Love only has logic, only has meaning, when it takes the form of the cross."[7] Today, let your profound insights and understanding of love, compassion, and justice take the form of the cross in your community, workplace, or family.

→ Pray

Father, I recognize the importance of balancing orthodoxy and orthopraxy in my life. While I enjoy gaining knowledge, help me to put it into action in practical ways. Prompt me whenever I become too focused on intellectual pursuits and neglect real-world problems or my personal responsibilities.

---

7   Voskamp, *The Broken Way*, 109.

Day 35 Reflections:

Do you find yourself leaning more toward orthodoxy or orthopraxy? Why do you think this is the case?

What real-life issues have you postponed due to your intellectual pursuits?

How can you establish intentional limits or boundaries around your learning to make room for your practical needs or responsibilities?

➔ **Respond**

Go on an intellectual fast (i.e. break). Designate specific days to abstain from reading books, listening to podcasts, online videos, or engaging in study. Use this time to focus on addressing your tangible needs and responsibilities.

Silence and Solitude

And after he had dismissed the crowds, he went up on the mountain

by himself to pray. When evening came, he was there alone.

—Matthew 14:23

FIVES PULL AWAY FROM THE WORLD IN order to get their needs met—namely, to protect their objectivity and mental clarity, as well as to quell anxiety.[2] Moments of solitude are not just gifts but the air Fives breathe. In Peter Høeg's novel *Smilla's Sense of Snow*, the protagonist, Smilla, beautifully expresses this sentiment: "I feel the same way about solitude as some people feel about the blessing of the church. It's the light of grace for me. I never close my door behind me without the awareness that I am carrying out an act of mercy toward myself."[3]

> I have never found the companion that was so companionable as solitude.
>
> –Henry David Thoreau[1]

These "acts of mercy" that nourish the soul of a Five might look like sitting in quiet contemplation by the fire on a cold

---

1   Henry David Thoreau, *Walden* (New York: Thomas Y. Crowell & Company, 1910), 178.

2   Carver and Green, *What's Your Enneatype?* 95.

3   Peter Høeg, *Smilla's Sense of Snow: A Novel* (New York: Farrar, Straus and Giroux, 2010), 11.

day or going outside to commune with nature. It could include any number of solitary, self-care activities such as hiking, fishing, cooking, painting, gardening, scrapbooking, or even decluttering.

That said, it's crucial to remember that self-care can turn into *self-ish* care if Fives remain isolated. Unhealthy Fives tend to stay in isolation, while healthy ones use solitude to recharge so they can come back to the community with their whole selves. The theologian Richard Foster emphasizes that after periods of solitude, we should feel a renewed desire to connect with others, show attentiveness to their needs, and be more responsive to their feelings.[4] In other words, our alone time should not only provide rest for our souls but also fuel a renewed energy to care for others.

To avoid using our times of solitude toward selfish ends, we need to practice *soul-care*—nurturing our souls in the One who makes us whole.

> Productive thinking comes from a peaceful soul.

This must include the practice of *silence,* for solitude in and of itself is insufficient.[5] Even if you manage to escape the crowd, you still have to find a way to quiet your racing mind. Fives often attempt to use their head to alleviate their fear and anxiety, but this strategy doesn't always work, as the "monkey mind"—that state of restlessness or insomnia where thoughts jump incessantly from one to another—keeps these moments of privacy from offering their full potential.

When you consent to the practice of silence, you are granting yourself the freedom to quiet the mental chatter and find peace in God's presence. The psalmist's command leading to peace is, "Be still, and know that I am God,"[6] because you can't really *know* God unless your mind is still. A peaceful soul isn't cultivated by more thinking. Rather, productive thinking comes from a peaceful soul. So, adopt a posture of listening today, allowing yourself to be led by the voice of the Holy Spirit who will guide you when you can't think your way out of

---

4   Richard J. Foster, *Celebration of Discipline: The Path to Spiritual Growth* (New York: HarperCollins, 1988), 108.

5   Christopher L. Heuertz, *The Sacred Enneagram: Finding Your Unique Path to Spiritual Growth* (Grand Rapids, MI: Zondervan, 2016), 216-218.

6   Psalm 46:10

your anxiety. As a secure child of God, you can give your mind a break and relax in uncertainty instead of constantly searching for the right answers.

The Good News for Investigators is that solitude isn't just a personal preference for Fives—it's a spiritual practice that aligns us with the rhythm of Jesus' life. As you carve out moments of quiet reflection, you are following in the footsteps of our Savior who often withdrew to lonely places to pray. You are also showing the church how to avoid noise and distractions, prioritize reflection and introspection, seek rest and rejuvenation, and commune with God through prayer. As you find solitude today, don't forget to practice body-mind silence as well, even if it's just for a few minutes. And like Smilla, don't forget to close the door without remembering that you are carrying out an act of mercy toward yourself.

→ Pray

Father, thank You for the example of Your Son, Jesus, who withdrew to lonely places to pray. Quiet my racing mind and help me rest in Your presence. Give me the ability to discern between healthy solitude and unhealthy isolation. May my solitude be a source of renewal, leading me to engage the world with good works.

Day 36 Reflections:

Which self-care activities bring you the most joy? Which ones require the least mental effort?

How does the concept of "monkey mind" resonate with you? When do you notice your thoughts jumping from one topic to another, causing restlessness?

When do you realize that self-care has become selfishness? What signs or indicators do you notice?

➜ Respond

Practice the discipline of silence right now by intentionally pausing your thoughts for a few minutes and listening for God's voice. After, jot down any insights or feelings you experienced during this time of quiet reflection.

Day 37:

The Engaged Parent

I am reminded of your sincere faith, a faith that dwelt first in your grandmother

Lois and your mother Eunice and now, I am sure, dwells in you as well.

—2 Timothy 1:5

INVESTIGATORS MAKE EXCEPTIONAL PARENTS, GRANDPARENTS, CAREGIVERS, AND mentors. They find joy when children and mentees seek their wisdom, and they relish the "why" stage, when children's curiosity leads to endless questions. Tracy Tresidder, Margaret Loftus, and Jacqui Pollock, authors of *Knowing Me Knowing Them*, explain the tremendous gifts that a Five parent brings:

> To be in your children's memories tomorrow, you have to be in their lives today.
>
> —Barbara Johnson[1]

"You are kind and devoted—your family can depend on your commitment to them. You can be grounded and keep things in perspective. You see the big picture for your family and don't get drawn into the drama. You have a brilliant mind and love learning for its own sake,

---

1   Barbara Johnson, *The Best Devotions of Barbara Johnson* (Grand Rapids, MI: Zondervan, 2010), 109.

and this encourages your children to have enquiring minds. You enjoy being wise and increasing your knowledge, and so can become a reliable resource for your children. You are self-sufficient and self-contained: you do not project your needs onto your children. You're very good at observing and can consider your responses without overreacting."[2]

Although Fives excel in the areas above, parenting can become stressful for several reasons, especially for stay-at-home or work-from-home parents. Children don't often respect personal boundaries and may interrupt you multiple times a day, leaving you vulnerable and emotionally raw. Prolonged social interactions can be very draining, not to mention being exposed to excessive emotions that you can't detach from, so you may shut down when situations are simply beyond your control or find it stressful when your teenager calls your competence into question.[3]

While every parent will fail many times in their attempts to steward the lives they've been charged with, there are unique ways a Five— particularly one in stress—can negatively affect those they love. They can sometimes exhibit authoritarian tendencies or come across as intellectually arrogant, leaving their children feeling judged or intimidated. Additionally, their need for privacy and space can lead them to miss out on experiences that are important to their child. Children of Five parents have noted that a lack of presence, or even a silent presence, can be interpreted as the parent not being interested in them. [4]

> Even when being a parent is tiring, God will give you the energy you need.

Tresidder, Loftus, and Pollock go on to offer some strategies to stay healthy and keep growing. First, instead of retreating into your mind and personal space, allow yourself to experience feelings and engage with your family more actively. Practice engaging in small talk with your children, showing genuine interest in their daily conversations. Being fully present in these interactions is crucial

---

2   Tracy Tresidder, Margaret Loftus, and Jacqui Pollock, *Knowing Me, Knowing Them: Understand Your Parenting Personality by Discovering the Enneagram* (Carlton North, Victoria, Australia: Monterey Press, 2014), 100-101.

3   Ibid., 103-104.

4   Ibid., 101-103.

for your children to feel heard and valued. Real-life connections often emerge between the lines, so focus on understanding their stories rather than dissecting them. Finally, manage your energy levels effectively, recognizing your need for alone time while also ensuring that your children feel included and supported. Be honest about your need for space, but be mindful of using it as a means to avoid important interactions of life events. The key is to *stay engaged*. Showing interest and communicating often will speak volumes.

As we look to the Bible, we find King David thriving in his career as a military and political leader, but struggling to stay engaged at home. Amnon, Absalom, Adonijah, and Solomon all faced challenges and made poor decisions, in part, because of their absent father. However, as we look to the New Testament, we find Timothy's mother, Eunice, offers a vastly different legacy as a parent. Eunice is deeply involved in Timothy's life, imparting wisdom and nurturing him to excel. She inherited a sincere faith from her mother, Lois, both of whom played a vital role in teaching Timothy the Scriptures.[5]

The Good News for Investigators is that, even when being a parent is tiring, God will give you the energy you need. As the psalmist reassures us, "My flesh and my heart may fail, but God is the strength of my heart and my portion forever."[6] Rest assured that in moments of weakness or fatigue as a parent, God is always there, ready to sustain you. With His help, you can be the engaged and loving parent your children need, even when things seem overwhelming. He's got you covered. And if it's any consolation, my mother says that it's much easier to be a Type Five grandparent than a parent. Hang in there!

→ Pray

Father, forgive me for the times I've responded with impatience or arrogance, and for allowing my need for privacy to create distance. Teach me to be present, to listen, and to find the balance between solitude and connection. Let my greatest achievement be offering children my loving presence just as You have done for me.

---

5   2 Timothy 1:5; 3:14-15

6   Psalm 73:26

Day 37 Reflections:

How have your unique strengths positively influenced the children in your life?

Which strategy for growth would you like to work on improving this week?

What opportunities are there in your home, extended family, or church community to teach and model the gospel for children or teens?

→ Respond

If you are a parent, schedule a consistent weekly "date" with each of your children. Let them pick the place and activity. If you aren't a parent, look for an opportunity to come alongside a family this week and offer your support.

Join the Dance

And let us consider how to stir up one another to love and good works,

not neglecting to meet together, as is the habit of some, but encouraging

one another, and all the more as you see the Day drawing near.

—Hebrews 10:24-25

IN THE BEGINNING, THE CREATOR SAID TO the darkness, "Let there be light."[2] Hovering above the waters of uncreated chaos, God imagined new possibilities and began painting, sculpting, and singing creation into existence. With His unfathomable knowledge and limitless power, rocks, animals, trees, mathematical formulas, scientific laws, and sexuality were written into existence. But the act of creation—and its ongoing enterprise—was always intended to be a community project: "Let *us* make man in *our* image … ."[3]

> God is ... a dynamic, pulsating activity, a life, almost a kind of drama ... a kind of dance.
>
> –C.S. Lewis[1]

---

1   C. S. Lewis, *Mere Christianity* (New York: Harper Collins, 2001) 174-176.

2   Genesis 1:3

3   Genesis 1:26 (author emphasis added)

C.S. Lewis beautifully captures the essence of this Trinitarian community and its importance for Investigators in his book *Mere Christianity*. He writes, "The whole dance, or drama, or pattern of this three-Personal life is to be played out in each one of us. … There is no other way to the happiness for which we were made."[4] Lewis explains that if you want to get warm, you have to stand near the fire. If you want to get wet, you have to jump into the water. In other words, the dynamic, pulsating activity of God's joy, power, peace, and eternal life is *caught*, not taught.

To join this dance and truly experience the richness of life, Fives must step out of hiding.[5] Average to unhealthy Investigators tend to stay in the shadows to avoid the complexities of social interaction, often keeping one foot in the room and the other out the door. Perfectly content to remain hidden, opaque, or on the periphery, they find safety in anonymity and in failing to be noticed.[6] But healthy Fives emerge from the shadows and embrace the light, much like thriving plants groping toward the sun. Just as plants undergo photosynthesis to convert light into energy, these Fives transform the communal light they receive into reserves of energy, rather than allowing it to sap their strength.

Conversely, when they stay in the shadows too long, hope begins to fail and feelings of cynicism grow. They become deeply disappointed when their ideal of a perfect union with another person proves unattainable or when relationships fall short of their expectations. Decision-making gets more difficult because all arguments start to feel equally valid or invalid, and therefore useless.[7] If the downward spiral continues, nihilism can creep in, leading to doubts about meaning, purpose, or whether there is any value in life. Some may even fall into the trap of conspiratorial thinking, supported by a mindset that you can't trust

---

4   Lewis, *Mere Christianity*, 176-177.

5   Ibid., 176-177.

6   Wagner, *Nine Lenses on the World*, 304.

7   Riso and Hudson, *Personality Types*, 197.

anyone in this world. All of these may lead Fives to agree with Solomon, the teacher of Ecclesiastes, and proclaim that "Everything is meaningless."[8]

Looking back, there were a lot of legitimate reasons for first-century Christians to feel hopeless and cynical. They were persecuted and oppressed by both Jewish and Roman authorities and experienced many in-house disagreements and divisions about theological and social issues. As a result, some grew disillusioned with their faith and retreated to the shadows, distancing themselves from their community and disengaging from these growing pains. This disengagement is largely why the author of Hebrews strongly exhorted the believers not to neglect meeting together, as many were doing at the time, but to gather for encouragement and support.[9] The author wanted these believers to know that community, not isolation, was the antidote to their discouragement. Likewise, Fives must remember that the church is not just the hope of the world but *their* hope too.

The Good News for Investigators is that we're not merely observers, but "partakers of the divine nature,"[10] participants in the ongoing creation of the world, invited to join the dance that has been happening since the dawn of time. Hoping to find life outside of the Triune Godhead only leads to a feeling of emptiness, thirst, and despair, but stepping into this community is like finding an oasis in the desert. Dive into these healing, refreshing waters of life.

➔ Pray

Father, when I isolate myself for too long, I can become cynical and withdrawn. But You, Lord, are my light in the darkness. Help me remember that true growth happens when I step into the light to be fully known and fully loved by You and others. Thank You for inviting me to join the dance of life with You.

---

8   Ecclesiastes 1:2 NIV

9   Hebrews 10:24-25

10   2 Peter 1:4

Day 38 Reflections:

How do you attempt to remain invisible or hidden in the shadows?

What fears or obstacles are still keeping you from engaging in social interactions or joining community gatherings?

Reflect on how Lewis' metaphor of "the dance" matches the language often used of the Trinity. If that is the way the Godhead relates within itself, how can it help you become more active within your community?

> ➜ **Respond**
>
> During your next social event, try staying twenty or thirty minutes longer than you normally would even if it feels wasteful or uncomfortable. After, take some time to reflect on your experience and what you learned from it.[11]

11   Moser, *The Enneagram of Discernment*, 319-320.

Day 39:

We're All Connected

But as it is, God arranged the members in the body, each one

of them, as he chose. If all were a single member, where would

the body be? As it is, there are many parts, yet one body.

—1 Corinthians 12:18-20

AS WE'VE COVERED OFTEN IN THESE LAST weeks, Investigators value independence and self-sufficiency above nearly all else: a trait that can be helpful in many instances but also carries the risk of isolation and loneliness.

> A person is a person through other persons; you can't be a human in isolation; you are human only in relationships.
>
> –Desmond Tutu[1]

The metaphor of the body of Christ, as used by the apostle Paul, can help them reorient their lives. Paul emphasizes that we are "all baptized into one body,"[2] meaning when we become Christians, we are part of something greater than ourselves. As a pastor, when my fellow introverts expressed a desire to be baptized in secret, I reminded them that baptism is

---

1   Chestnut and Paes, *The Enneagram Guide to Waking Up*, 121.

2   1 Corinthians 12:13

not a solitary act but is rather a communal celebration of our shared faith and journey. This applies to all significant milestones, like birthdays, quinceañeras, and graduations. Others want to share in your joy because they feel connected to you, and your victories feel like their victories too.

Stepping into *healthy interdependence* can be challenging, especially for Fives who cherish their privacy and routines. Typically, their routine is well-planned and actively followed each day: wake up at the same time, make coffee, read their Bible, journal, check that to-do list, go to work, come home, watch their favorite show, read a book, and go to bed at a specific time. Suzanne Stabile says, "With a schedule like that, imagine the challenge of integrating other people and their needs."[3]

Yet, if Fives are willing to give up some of their time and privacy to make themselves more available (as unappealing as that may sound), they bring a unique gift to the body of Christ. Investigators see the world in high definition—much like our body's visual system, they are wonderfully made to pick up on details the rest of us miss. Just as our eyes help us understand the world around us, Fives' keen observation and analytical skills bring insight and wisdom to their communities. When their observations and thoughts are shared, it helps everyone see things more clearly and understand the world better.

> Depending on others isn't a sign of weakness, but a display of trust in God's sufficiency.

As you stretch yourself to be more generous and spontaneous with your time and gifts, remember that healthy interdependence also requires you to *lean on* others a bit more: "The eye cannot say to the hand, 'I have no need of you.'"[4] While this can be very difficult at first, you must remind yourself that depending on others isn't a sign of weakness, but a display of trust in God's sufficiency. Independence is valuable, but Fives sometimes overestimate its importance, seeing it as vital for their survival. Paul's metaphor suggests otherwise: we can't thrive without the support of others. In fact, a study revealed that people with strong social

---

3   Suzanne Stabile, *The Path Between Us: An Enneagram Journey to Healthy Relationships* (Downers Grove, IL: InterVarsity Press, 2018), 131-132.

4   1 Corinthians 12:21

connections have a 50% higher chance of survival compared to those with weaker or fewer social connections. Healthy relationships are a literal lifesaver![5]

The first and perhaps the "easiest" step toward depending on others is to accept help when it's offered. Surprisingly, there are people who genuinely want to serve you without any hidden agenda! Yes, there are manipulative individuals out there with ulterior motives, yet the truth remains that you also have people who care and sincerely see you as a blessing, not a burden. There are loved ones who don't view your needs as disruptions but as opportunities to grow closer to you. So, the next time someone offers assistance, advice, emotional support, or even financial help, the best and most humble response is simply, "Thank you, I need it!"

The Good News for Investigators is that Christ holds all of us together. We have good heads on our shoulders, and as Paul says, "we are to grow up in every way into him who is the head, into Christ, from whom the whole body, joined and held together by every joint with which it is equipped, when each part is working properly, makes the body grow so that it builds itself up in love."[6]

Let this redefine your understanding of self-sufficiency. It's not about measuring our worth or capabilities but about leaning on God and one another. In a world and culture that often celebrates individualism, let us remember that connectedness brings wholeness and implies responsibility. When every part gives itself away, life fills the body, and love abounds.

→ Pray

Father, give me the courage to break free from my routines and be more available to support others. I admit it's challenging to lean on others, but help me understand that depending on them is an act of trust in Your sufficiency. Thank You for putting people in my life who want to help. I will strive to accept their assistance with humility and gratitude.

---

5   Julianne Holt-Lunstad, Timothy B Smith, Mark Baker, Tyler Harris, and David Stephenson, "Loneliness and Social Isolation as Risk Factors for Mortality: A Meta-Analytic Review." *Perspectives on Psychological Science* 10, no. 2 (2015): 227–237. doi:10.1177/1745691614568352.

6   Ephesians 4:15-16

Day 39 Reflections:

How comfortable are you with depending on others? Why do you find it challenging?

Can you recall a time when you resisted accepting help from someone? What were the reasons behind your refusal?

In what ways can you change your daily routine to make yourself more available to others? Who in your life could benefit from more support or encouragement from you?

→ Respond

Get involved in edifying the local church body by signing up to become a Bible study leader, Sunday school teacher, research or sermon prep assistant, library curator, audio-visual volunteer, mentor, or find another way that resonates with you. Don't hoard your knowledge or skills, but seek to give them away!

Your Place in History

Therefore, since we are surrounded by so great a cloud of witnesses,

let us also lay aside every weight, and sin which clings so closely,

and let us run with endurance the race that is set before us...

—Hebrews 12:1

ONE INVESTIGATOR WHO FEARLESSLY LEFT HIS MARK in history was the Renaissance polymath Leonardo Da Vinci. His introverted nature allowed him to delve deeply into his studies and follow his curiosities without seeking fame and riches. Remarkably, he left behind over seven thousand pages of observations and research, yet much about his personal life remains a mystery. While his *Mona Lisa* and *The Last Supper* are artistic masterpieces, painting was just one aspect of his vast contributions. Da Vinci dissected cadavers and studied anatomy, producing countless accurate scientific drawings for future generations.

> One of the worst things you can die with is potential. Die with failures before you die with potential.
>
> —Henry Cloud[1]

---

1 Henry Cloud, *9 Things You Simply Must Do to Succeed in Love and Life: a Psychologist Probes the Mystery of Why Some Lives Really Work and Others Don't* (Nashville, TN: Thomas Nelson, 2006), 41.

His daring designs for flying machines, like the ornithopter and parachute, foreshadowed inventions that wouldn't become reality for centuries.[2]

Da Vinci stands as a shining example for all Investigators, showing how history can be shaped by those who are willing to step out of their comfort zones. He embraced experimentation and innovation, pushed boundaries, and fearlessly pursued his interests, even in the face of skepticism or criticism. This is crucial because many Fives see themselves as merely tiny specks in the vast universe. In one sense, this is quite true: we are one species dwelling on a small planet, orbiting a small star in a modestly-sized system, within an average galaxy, among billions of others in a rapidly-expanding universe. However, that view is far too modest. You are yourself not a speck, but a planet whose life and work contain multitudes. Though you may feel disconnected at times from the whole, you are not an isolated wanderer but a member of the cosmic dance. This means whatever you're doing right now, no matter how seemingly small or insignificant, has the power to resonate across millions of miles or millennia.

> Whatever a Five does privately in their study can resonate and impact the wider world.

Take a moment to consider what God is nudging you toward. Where is your curiosity taking you? What new discoveries do you long to make? Is there a field of study you're passionate about that hasn't been fully explored? How can you carve out a unique niche, challenge conventional wisdom, or push the boundaries? What ingenious invention, revolutionary piece of technology, captivating novel, or thought-provoking film is the world eagerly anticipating from you? What's one thing you'd absolutely love to accomplish, but seems beyond reach without God's intervention?

When a Five reaches their highest level of development, they become filled with confidence, self-assurance, and aren't afraid of anyone.[3] They cultivate a sense of agency, owning their power and becoming more assertive, suddenly coming to

---

2   Ledys Chemin and Giordana Goretti. "The Enneagram Types in Art – of Amazing Painters, Paintings and Diagrams." DailyArt Magazine, May 29, 2024. https://www.dailyartmagazine.com/enneagram-types-of-artists/.

3   In Enneagram theory, as Fives move along their growth line to Type Eight, they adopt the healthy characteristics of that type.

realize their knowledge actually *is* power. Don't underestimate what you have to offer, and when it comes to planning the next thing, don't overthink it but trust your gut. When it comes to your beliefs and values, stand up for them. Don't shy away from a good debate whenever it presents itself. As Dr. Jerome Wagner encourages Fives: climb up on the soapbox instead of hiding under it.[4]

The world needs to see your brilliance and what you are capable of, but don't delay. As the psalmist wisely noted, time is limited, and we need to use it wisely: "So teach us to number our days that we may get a heart of wisdom."[5]

The Good News for Investigators is "we are surrounded by so great a cloud of witnesses."[6] The author of Hebrews recounts the stories of those who lived by faith rather than for their own security. Inspired by these spiritual giants, whose shoulders we now stand on, we are encouraged to "lay aside every weight, and sin which clings so closely, and let us run with endurance the race that is set before us … ."[7] Throughout this entire book, I've aimed to shed light on the unique challenges that may be holding you back as a Five. My hope now is that you would learn to release those burdens, enabling you to run faster and farther in the exciting story God has written just for you. Thank you for embarking on this forty-day journey with me. You are truly a fascinating and intriguing human, and I can't wait to see what the world will learn from you next!

→ Pray

Father, help me remember that I am not merely a tiny speck in the vast universe. Empower me to grow in confidence, self-assurance, and agency in my life. Guide me as I plan for the future, trusting in the abilities You have given me. Thank You for leading me on this forty-day journey. I am excited to see where You will take me next.

---

4   Wagner, *Nine Lenses on the World*, 327-328.

5   Psalm 90:12

6   Hebrews 12:1

7   Hebrews 12:1

Day 40 Reflections:

Reflecting on your journey, what accomplishments are you proud of and what have you been affirmed for the most?

What new discoveries, fields of study, or innovative ideas do you feel drawn to explore next? What is one thing you'd absolutely love to accomplish, but seems beyond reach without God's intervention?

How do you want the world to remember you?

→ **Respond**

Find a life coach, spiritual mentor, or counselor to come alongside and support you in accomplishing your goals. Start working courageously toward something today that seems impossible without God's supernatural power and grace.

Prayer for Investigators

Father, I am deeply grateful to You for creating me in Your image as Your beloved child. You created me specifically to reflect Your curiosity, wisdom, and truth. I confess that my insatiable need for knowledge has often led me to live inside my head rather than take action. I have found myself being reclusive, uncommunicative, self-reliant, and cynical at times. But You, being rich in mercy, saw me from heaven and sent Your Son, Jesus, to die on the cross when I was leaning on my own understanding and depending on no one but myself. Now I revel in the fact that I can completely depend on You, and through You, the community placed around me. My needs are not a problem. Rather, when clothed with the power of Your Holy Spirit, I will embrace my emotions as an asset, remembering that I'm not a "thinking head on a stick" but a human being with deep desires and a need for connection. Help me to put off my self-sufficiency and stinginess and put on my new self, made in Christ's image. Guide me as I pursue relationships over isolation, wearing my heart on my sleeve and living life to the fullest, rather than observing it from a safe distance.

Three Types of Investigators

Below is a summary of the three types of Fives (called subtypes) from the teaching of Beatrice Chestnut, whose book, *The Complete Enneagram*, covers all 27 subtypes of the main nine Enneagram types.[1] As discussed in the introduction, these subtypes help us drill down the different nuances of the Investigator.

Warning: many of these descriptions will seem overly negative. However, one of the main purposes of the Enneagram is to help us discover our "shadow self"— the ways we interact with the world unconsciously and in times of stress. These descriptions are not indictments; rather, they are a further opportunity to deepen our awareness of how we naturally interact with the world and ways to make healthier choices for ourselves and those around us.

The Self-Preservation Five

The Self-Preservation Five is the most private of the subtypes and the clearest example of introversion. Often called the "castle," they feel a need to hide behind thick, protected walls in order to have a safe sanctuary from a world that can seem hostile, needy, and demanding. They can be the loners of the Enneagram, avoiding social contact and pressures through solitude, privacy, and setting clearly defined boundaries to recharge. They are true survivalists: fearing to become too dependent on others, they learn how to live inside their castle walls by denying or reducing their physical and emotional needs. This often looks like sacrificing their desires and living on very little, using their resourcefulness to preserve what they do have, and convincing themselves they don't really need anything else—including the support of others. Though they are the least expressive and communicative of all the Fives, they let down their drawbridge of genuine warmth and humor to a few trusted people in their lives. This subtype is the most classic Five and unlikely to be mistaken for any other type.

The Social Five

The Social Five is someone who passionately pursues knowledge and secretly wants to be seen and recognized as the wise expert in their circle of friends and colleagues. Their thirst for knowledge and time spent learning is often used as a

---

1   Chestnut, *The Complete Enneagram*.

substitute for and distraction from the benefits of direct human contact. Fearing that life is meaningless, they chase after ultimate ideals to connect them to something meaningful that will elevate their life. To this end, they pursue and surround themselves with admired experts who share their intellectual values and interests, but can be cold and less attentive toward the "regular" people in their life. Due to their intellectualizing approach, they may find ways to bypass the difficult work of spiritual transformation, believing that simply thinking through the needed changes is sufficient. This subtype may often look like Sevens because they can be outgoing and display excitement when talking to interesting people about their ideas; however, they are more reserved, less emotional overall, and less self-interested than typical Sevens.

The One-to-One Five

The One-to-One Five is the "countertype" who looks a lot like the other Fives on the surface, but underneath is emotionally sensitive, intensely imaginative, and in touch with their desires. They have a vibrant inner life that is highly romantic, like a Four, but primarily display their emotions through some medium of self-expression, such as art. Whereas the other Fives seek a connection to knowledge and ideals, this Five goes on a search for intimacy, longing for a perfect union with another person. This can be fulfilled through a love interest or by pursuing deep one-on-one connections with a few friends they share chemistry with. They can be relationally picky, idealizing others whom they want to be fully transparent with and loved by, despite their flaws, but are often disappointed when those relationships don't meet their expectations. Trust is of utmost importance, and these Fives may test their loved ones to shake off the fear of being hurt. Once trust is built, these Fives are life-long confidants who will keep all your secrets and expect the same of you. Although this Five may mistype as a Four, they are more detached from their feelings and fear depletion more than being defective.

Next Steps

I'm so proud of you for finishing this 40-day journey. That's a big accomplishment! Though this book isn't small by any means, you may feel (like me) that we've only begun to explore the tip of the iceberg. You're probably wondering: *What now? My eyes have been opened, I've grown in greater self-awareness and empathy, and now I'm ready to take the next step!* Here are some ideas:

1. Follow "Gospel for Enneagram" on Instagram, YouTube, Facebook, or Twitter to continue learning and engaging.

2. Download my free resource called *Should Christians Use The Enneagram?* at gospelforenneagram.com.

3. If you found this book helpful, please leave an honest review (or star rating) online or share on social media so others can find it.

4. Visit my website, gospelforenneagram.com, to find more helpful links and resources.

5. Join a church community where you can continue to grow in your knowledge of God and self. To go the distance, find a mentor, coach, or support system.

6. Ask a friend, spouse, or mentor to meet regularly with you to discuss the insights God has revealed to you through this book. Invite them, along with your small group, to get a devotional on their Enneagram type and share what they learn with you.

7. Email me with any thoughts, questions, or feedback at tyler@gospelforenneagram.com. I'd love to hear from you!

Acknowledgements

My wife: Lindsey, you show me the gospel every day by loving me for who I am and not what I do. Thank you for your tremendous encouragement to be a writer and for bearing with my workaholic tendencies. I want to be more like you.

My editors: Joshua, thank you for bringing your incredible creativity to the table. Your re-rewrites helped elevate my writing to a whole new level. Stephanie, your attention to detail and passion for this project gave me tremendous confidence. Lee Ann, your veteran experience and thoroughness increased the value of this book tenfold. And finally, I want to express my heartfelt gratitude to my mother, Kim. She dedicated countless weeks to meticulously vetting this book, ensuring it resonates even more deeply with you. Her unwavering support and daily reminders to "get to the point faster" have been invaluable in clarifying my message!

My coach: John Fooshee, thank you for your Enneagram coaching and partnership. I'm deeply grateful for your willingness to come alongside me and put wind in my sails.

My influences: I wouldn't have been able to pull this off without a multitude of direct and indirect influences such as pastors, teachers, and writers (including you, mom!) over the years. I'm deeply grateful for the spiritual heroes who have come before me and shaped me.

www.GospelForEnneagram.com

Follow us:

 /GospelForEnneagram

 @GospelForEnneagram

 @GospelForGram

 Gospel For Enneagram